YOU DO YOU

FIGURING OUT YOUR BODY, DATING, AND SEXUALITY

SARAH MIRK

TWENTY-FIRST CENTURY BOOKS / MINNEAPOLIS

THIS BOOK IS DEDICATED TO TILLIE AND KIT,
WHO HAVE TO GROW UP IN THIS WORLD.

Twenty-First Century Books
An imprint of Lerner Publishing Group, Inc.
241 First Avenue North
Minneapolis, MN 55401 USA

For reading levels and more information, look up this title
at www.lernerbooks.com.

Main body text set in Adrianna Condensed 11/15. Typeface provided by Chank.

Library of Congress Cataloging-in-Publication Data

Names: Mirk, Sarah, author.
Title: You do you : figuring out your body, dating, and sexuality / by Sarah Mirk.
Description: Minneapolis : Twenty-First Century Books, [2019] | Includes
    bibliographical references and index. |
Identifiers: LCCN 2018040394 (print) | LCCN 2018042116 (ebook) |
    ISBN 9781541562714 (eb pdf) | ISBN 9781541540224 (lb : alk. paper)
Subjects: LCSH: Sex—Juvenile literature. | Teenagers—Sexual behavior—Juvenile
    literature. | Dating (Social customs)—Juvenile literature. | Adolescence—
    Juvenile literature.
Classification: LCC HQ35 (ebook) | LCC HQ35 .M59155 2019 (print) | DDC
    306.70835—dc23
LC record available at https://lccn.loc.gov/2018040394

Manufactured in the United States of America
1-45227-36609-5/2/2019

CONTENTS

CHAPTER ONE
YOUR BODY, YOUR RULES   4

CHAPTER TWO
THERE IS NO NORMAL   13

CHAPTER THREE
MACHO MEN AND GIRLY GIRLS   30

CHAPTER FOUR
TAKE CARE DOWN THERE   44

CHAPTER FIVE
KNOW YOUR GERMS   53

CHAPTER SIX
TALKING ABOUT FEELINGS   61

CHAPTER SEVEN
DO WHAT FEELS GOOD   75

CHAPTER EIGHT
YOU DESERVE TO BE HAPPY   94

GLOSSARY   106

SOURCE NOTES   109

SELECTED BIBLIOGRAPHY   111

FURTHER INFORMATION   112

INDEX   117

CHAPTER ONE
YOUR BODY, YOUR RULES

The first thing to know about your body is that it's yours. You get to decide what to do with your body—what it looks like, what feels good, what feels bad, and who to share it with and how. That may sound super obvious, but it's actually the basis of a big idea that's the foundation of all dating and sexuality: consent.

Consent refers to granting permission for something to happen or agreeing to do something. When it comes to your body, consent is crucial. If someone's going to touch your body, they need your permission. If you're going to touch someone else's body, you need their permission. If you don't like the way someone touches you, talks to you, or makes you feel, you have the right to tell them to treat you differently. Establishing boundaries and making sure they're respected is hard work. But everyone, including you, has the right to be happy, healthy, and respected.

WHAT'S IMPORTANT TO YOU?

How do you decide what you want to do with your body? How do you decide what to wear? How to spend your free time? Who to kiss? Who to date? Who to have sex with? Whether to kiss, date, or have sex with anyone at all? The answers to these giant, complicated questions come from you and your values.

Values are the set of principles that define the way you want to be in the world. They guide not just what you do but what you believe. Values come from all parts of your life—from your family, your friends, your culture, and your communities. Sometimes these values match your feelings and beliefs perfectly. Sometimes they don't. If they don't, you have the right to question them and to shape your values in a way that makes sense for you. If you find yourself questioning the values of people in your life, look for people who share values closer to yours and talk to them. You get to pick what values feel most important to you and what defines the absolute core of who you are. You define your values for yourself.

Not everyone has the same values. What's important to you is not the same as what's important to everyone else. Recognizing that difference is essential for helping you make decisions and understanding the decisions other people make. Whenever you face a difficult situation, it's helpful to ask, "Well, what choice is most in line with my values?"

Figuring out your values requires examining the big ideas behind your desires. Here are some examples. Do any of these describe what's most important to you? Make a list of your core values. Here are some ideas to get started:

- living an independent life
- respecting privacy and personal choices
- exploring the world as much as possible
- respecting my parents' wishes
- supporting my family
- being a compassionate friend
- behaving as my religion tells me to

- making the world a better place
- doing whatever makes me happy
- living sustainably, so I impact the environment as little as possible
- being honest about my life with my family and friends
- taking care of my body and health above all else
- working as hard as possible to be the absolute best

SCENARIOS: WE WANT DIFFERENT THINGS

Explore contrasting values in these two scenarios:

Elyse and Jessie go to the homecoming dance. The DJ plays a song that Elyse hates—it's about how men only like women with big butts. She thinks it's demeaning to women. But to her surprise, Jessie runs out on the dance floor and starts dancing along. She loves the song! She seems to have fun dancing in a super-sexy way that shocks Elyse, who feels left out and abandoned. When the song is over, Elyse tells Jessie that she was dancing like a total idiot. Jessie feels really hurt and starts crying.

- What values might Elyse have that make her not want to participate in dancing along to this song?
- What values might Jessie have that make her feel good about dancing to this song?
- How could Jessie and Elyse have handled this situation differently to be true to themselves but not hurt each other?

Amisa has been accepted to two colleges: her dream school in Los Angeles, where she could pursue her passion of filmmaking, and the more affordable state school nearby. Her boyfriend is going to the state school too. If she goes there, they could stay together and maybe get married soon. Her parents, who are paying for half the cost of college, also want her to go to the state school because it will be cheaper. Amisa is wondering whether she should take out bigger student loans and leave her boyfriend so she can follow her ambition to be a film director.

- What values are important to Amisa?
- What will she be sacrificing by making either decision?
- What pressures is she facing? Which should she take seriously, and which should she maybe ignore?

CALL OUT CATCALLING

"Hey sexy!" "Nice butt!" "I'd hit that!" One of the most common examples of consent violating is street harassment. The group Stop Street Harassment defines gender-based street harassment as any unwanted comments, gestures, and actions forced on a stranger in a public place without their consent and directed at them because of their actual or perceived sex, gender, gender expression, or sexual orientation. Street harassment involves someone leering, whistling, honking, making a sexist comment, calling out a slur, following you, or blocking your path. In the United States, 65 percent of women and 25 percent of men have experienced some form of sexual harassment. Lesbian, gay, bisexual, transgender, and queer/questioning (LGBTQ) people face higher rates of harassment. People often try to brush off street harassment by saying it's a compliment or "just a joke." But it's not okay to make sexual comments to anyone without their permission.

YOUR BODY, YOUR RULES

Consent is linked to values. You get to make rules about your body. And it's also your job to respect other people's decisions about what they want for their bodies. That means listening to what they like or don't like. It also means listening to what they're *not* saying and paying close attention to their body language.

Consent is the foundation of all good relationships—friendships, professional situations, dating, marriage, and interacting with strangers. Consent requires communication. That means clearly agreeing (out loud or in writing) to whatever is going on. Consent takes the place of making assumptions about how another person is feeling. You often don't know! Or you get it wrong.

SCENARIO: BROKEN TRUST

Here is an example of friends working out consent:

> *Byron and Kelly are good friends who are in art class together. For his final project, Byron takes some artistic photos of parts of his body that he doesn't usually show people—his chest, his stomach, and his butt. Kelly says she'd love to see the project, so he emails her the photos and she gives him some feedback. He asks her to delete the photos after she's seen them because he doesn't want other people to see them or for them to wind up online. Kelly does exactly that, deleting the photos without showing them to anyone else.*

Byron communicated his boundaries in clear words: it was okay for Kelly to see these photos but no one else. He was trusting her to respect his rules. He didn't just send her the photos out of the blue. Sending someone photos that could be perceived as sexual is something for which you always need consent first. If Kelly had forwarded the photos to other friends or posted them online, that would have violated Byron's consent. Kelly would have broken his trust.

THEIR BODY, THEIR RULES

In dating, it's super important to get someone's verbal consent before getting up in their personal space, touching their body, or touching them in a new way. Consent is checking in, with words, to make sure the person you're with is feeling good. One simple example of good consent comes from the 2013 Disney film *Frozen.* In a cute, romantic moment, hunky ice harvester Kristoff asks heroine Anna if he may kiss her. She leans in and kisses him on the cheek, replying that he may.

When you have permission to kiss someone, it's not a blanket permission to touch them anywhere you want.

> WHEN YOU HAVE PERMISSION TO KISS SOMEONE, IT'S NOT A BLANKET PERMISSION TO TOUCH THEM ANYWHERE YOU WANT.

Instead, if you want to touch their breasts or genitalia, you need to get consent, asking again, "Can I. . . ?" Another way to ask for consent is to offer to do something you want to do. For example, "I'd love to take your shirt off. Is that okay?" or "I want to do something nice for you. Can I give you a massage?"

Then you need to closely listen to what they say. If someone seems hesitant or uncertain, that's not consent. Consent needs to be certain. So take the cue and don't push. If you're the person giving consent, know that it's always okay to say no. No one is entitled to your body—not even your boyfriend, girlfriend, or long-term partner. And it's okay to change your mind and say no after you already said yes if something doesn't feel good or you just don't want to anymore.

The University of Michigan Sexual Assault Prevention and Awareness Center has this great guide to consent issues:

- **Appearance or clothing.** The way a person dresses, dances, or smiles doesn't give you permission to touch them without asking.
- **Relationship status.** Just because someone is your girlfriend or boyfriend doesn't mean they want to have sex with you.
- **Previous activity.** If you've had sex in the past, it doesn't mean you consent to all future sex. Same thing goes for kissing and anything else involving your body.
- **Silence, passivity, lack of resistance, or immobility.** A person's silence isn't consent. A person who does not respond to attempts to engage in sexual activity, even if they do not verbally say no or resist physically, is not clearly agreeing to sexual activity.
- **Incapacitation.** Alcohol consumption or use of other drugs can render a person incapable of giving consent. Alcohol is often used to target individuals and by perpetrators to excuse their own actions.

SCENARIO: MAKE SPACE TO LISTEN

Here is an example of people respecting consent in romantic relationships:

Margot and Alison hang out and make out whenever they can, but they haven't had sex. One weekend, Alison's parents are going out of town and she decides to invite Margot to stay the night. But Alison is nervous because she doesn't want to have sex—she doesn't feel emotionally ready. Via text, she asks Margot if she'd like to sleep over and adds that she would love to make out but isn't ready to have sex. Margot texts back, "Yes!! Of course! We can keep our shorts on." That weekend is great. They watch a movie, then make out. Margot makes sure to check in a few times and ask if Alison is cool with everything they're doing.

Consent relates to respecting values. Alison was able to communicate what was important to her, and Margot respected that, even if she would have liked to have sex. When Alison made her needs clear, Margot didn't get angry, tell her she was wrong, or try to convince her to change her mind. Instead, Alison established a clear ground rule that they could both understand.

Here is an example of an interaction where consent is violated:

Darren is sitting on the couch at a party when Latoya comes over and sits on his lap without asking. She wraps her arms around his neck and starts playing with his hair. It feels super flirty to Darren. He's embarrassed—he likes Latoya as a friend, but he's not attracted to her. He asks her to move off his lap and give him a little space, but she gets mad and says, "What? You don't want a girl on you? Are you gay?"

Latoya makes a pretty nasty accusation: that if Darren doesn't want her in his personal space, it must be because he's not attracted to women at all. This is both homophobic and rude. If Latoya wants to sit on Darren's lap, she needs to ask him first. If he says no, she needs to respect that decision without making any assumptions about his sexuality. What should she do now that she's violated his personal boundaries? What steps can Darren take to feel more okay after this interaction?

QUESTIONS TO THINK ABOUT

I made out with this guy I have a crush on at a party—I'm a sophomore and he's a senior who has a lot of friends and is really popular. I'm really into him. But after the party, he found me on Snapchat and sent me a photo of his dick! I didn't know what to do, so I just erased it. Then he sent me a message that said to send him a photo of my boobs. I don't want to, because I've heard about photos like that winding up online. But if I don't, he will probably lose interest in me and that could kill our chances of ever dating. Should I just send him a photo?

This guy violated your consent by sending you a photo of his penis without your requesting it. And now he's asking you to cross your own boundaries. Those are two big red flags. You wouldn't want someone to flash you their genitalia in public, and online is no different! You have good instincts here. Listen to yourself. Anything you send digitally can be downloaded, copied, and shared without your knowing about it. Don't send a sexy photo to someone you don't entirely trust. If a guy doesn't respect your right to privacy and your boundaries, he's not someone you want to date.

CHAPTER TWO
THERE IS NO NORMAL

The one thing humans around the world have in common is that every single one of us is different. So whether you're comparing height, weight, body hair, or breast size, what's normal for one person is not normal for another.

BELOW THE BELT

Just as no two humans have exactly the same personality, no two humans have exactly the same genitalia. Instead, reproductive and sexual organs come in many shapes and sizes. In the womb, every fetus starts out with the same genitalia. As the fetus grows, the cells that make up its genitalia shift around. Sex researcher Emily Nagoski says, "We're all made of the same parts, just organized in different ways."

Our reproductive and sexual organs serve three basic purposes:

- **Getting rid of waste.** Your genitals are where poop, pee, and menstrual fluid come out of your body. Yep.

- **Feeling good.** Human genitalia is hardwired to feel pleasure. It's full of nerve endings that send good vibes straight to your brain.
- **Making babies.** Babies are made when sperm (reproductive cells made in the testes) fertilize an egg, a large reproductive cell that's made in the ovaries. Sperm can get into the ovaries in a couple of different ways. One way is that a penis is inserted into the vulva. When the penis ejaculates, or releases, sperm in the vagina, the sperm swim up the vagina, through the cervix, and into the ovaries, where the sperm and egg can meet. This can also sometimes happen if sperm is ejaculated just on the lips of the vulva, not all the way inside. Fertilization can also happen through artificial insemination, when doctors collect sperm from one person and inject it into someone who wants to get pregnant.

Biological sex is based on someone's anatomy and hormones. In the United States, legally recognized sexes are male, female and, in some states, intersex and nonbinary. Gender identity is defined by you based on how you think about yourself. The most common gender descriptions are woman and man, but many people describe their gender as nonbinary, agender, genderqueer, and lots of other options.

When a baby is born, doctors and parents look at the baby's reproductive and sexual organs and its chromosomes and make a determination about the baby's sex. If a baby has testes, a penis, and XY chromosomes, it's classified as male. If a baby has a vulva, a womb, and XX chromosomes, it's classified as female. For the majority of people, the sex assigned at birth is the same as their gender identity. This is being cisgender. If someone's sex assigned at birth does not match their gender identity later in life, that's being transgender.

Sometimes, a baby has a different configuration of its internal and external anatomy. For example, a baby with testes and a penis may have XX chromosomes or a baby with XY chromosomes and a uterus may not have a vagina. Variations like these that do not fit into the binary definition of male or female bodies are intersex. The Intersex Society of North America estimates that about 1 in 1,500 or 1 in 2,000 babies are born with sexual anatomy variations. In the past, most doctors performed surgery on the genitalia of intersex babies to make the anatomy match the doctor's determination of a baby's sex. These surgeries often took place under a cloud of stigma and secrecy. Many intersex children did not even know they had had surgery at birth. These days, the Intersex Society of North America recommends that these surgeries not be performed on intersex children. They should be able to choose what they want when they are older and to give informed consent about their treatment. They should also have expert advice and peer support to make decisions.

VULVAS, UTERUSES, VAGINAS—OH MY!

Many people have misconceptions about what the word *vagina* refers to. Here's what is accurate: The vagina is a muscular and flexible internal canal that has a small external opening. The vaginal canal connects to the cervix and uterus. The outside part of this genitalia—the part you can see—is the vulva.

If you haven't ever looked at your genitalia, go for it! Get a handheld mirror and put it between your legs, angling it upward so you can see what's there. If you have a vulva, the first thing you'll probably see is hair. Pubic hair begins to grow on the labia majora (Latin for "big lips") during puberty. If you want to, you can carefully trim this hair with scissors to get a better look at your vulva. (Some people shave and wax pubic hair. But be careful if you decide to do this. You can end up with painful razor burn or ingrown hairs.) Inside the labia majora are smaller folds of skin called the labia minora, or "small lips." Both sets of lips help protect the vulva's supersensitive areas. The inner and outer lips of the vulva come in all shapes, sizes, and colors. They may be brown, pink, red, or purplish.

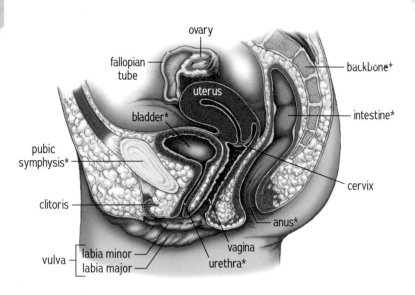

ovary

fallopian
tube

backbone*

uterus

bladder*

intestine*

pubic
symphysis*

cervix

clitoris

anus*

vagina

vulva — labia minor
labia major

urethra*

*not part of the reproductive system

Sex educator Heather Corinna describes the labia minora this way: "They tend to look a lot like flower petals or two little tongues."

Toward the backside of the vulva is the vaginal opening. This is the hole that people insert fingers, toys, or penises into when they want to have vaginal sex. The vaginal opening also is where to insert tampons if you menstruate. It's also where babies pass through during vaginal childbirth.

Inside is the vagina canal, a muscular tube 3 to 6 inches (7 to 15 cm) long that connects to the cervix and uterus. The uterus is where eggs, made in the ovaries, wait to be fertilized. If an egg is fertilized, that

VULVA MYTHS

Sometimes people joke that vulvas smell like fish. Vulvas do have a slight smell, but it's a normal, healthy smell. Vulvas are actually self-cleaning. Isn't that cool? But if you do notice that your vulva has a rotten or musky smell, you may have an infection. Make an appointment right away to see a doctor.

person becomes pregnant. If the egg is not fertilized, the egg and a layer of the uterus's internal lining flow out of the vagina for a few days once a month. That's menstruation, or a period.

A thin membrane called the hymen covers the entrance to the vaginal canal. Hymens are often naturally full of holes. Everyday activities such as bike riding, horseback riding, or gymnastics can rip the hymen. So if you decide to have vaginal sex someday, you may or may not have a hymen.

Above the vaginal opening is a much smaller hole that leads to the urethra—the hole that pee comes out of. This connects to your bladder. Inserting anything into the urethra is typically extremely painful, so steer clear if you're poking around.

At the top end of the vulva is the clitoris, a round and very sensitive organ. The clitoris is the vulva's pleasure center. It is home to eight thousand nerve endings. It doesn't have any reproductive function, so scientists think the whole point of the clitoris is to feel good. The visible part of the clitoris is often pea-size or even smaller and is part of a much larger internal organ.

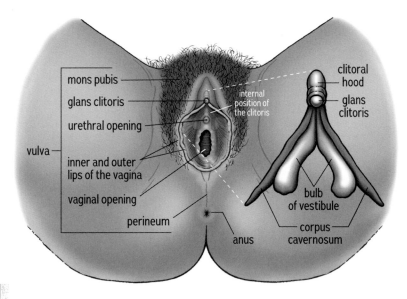

mons pubis

glans clitoris

urethral opening

vulva

inner and outer lips of the vagina

vaginal opening

perineum

internal position of the clitoris

clitoral hood

glans clitoris

bulb of vestibule

corpus cavernosum

anus

DICK-TIONARY

Penises are just as unique and varied as vulvas. The head of the penis is more sensitive than the shaft. Inside the shaft are long cylinders of tissue that are usually soft and spongy. When you're sexually stimulated, blood rushes to the penis and fills up the spongy tissue, making it hard. This is an erection. Erections are sometimes called boners, even though the penis actually has no bones. It's only tissue, and it softens again when the blood leaves.

The shaft and head of the penis are covered by the foreskin, a piece of stretchy skin. When the penis becomes erect, the foreskin naturally retracts, revealing the head. About 80 percent of Americans with penises have surgery to remove the foreskin, usually when they're babies. This circumcision is done for cultural or religious reasons or because parents believe foreskins contribute to health risks. The science on whether it's healthier to be circumcised or uncircumcised is hotly debated. Many critics say the surgery is unnecessary.

Penises are all shaped a little differently. Some are long, some are short, some are thick around, and some are skinny. Some penises are very straight when erect, and other penises curve up or down. People

BONER SCIENCE

Erections aren't controllable, and they don't happen just from sexual stimulation. Erections can happen if you see something that turns you on. But they also happen as a reflex reaction in situations where you get nervous, scared, angry, or stressed. A lot of people get erections when they least want them, like right before a class presentation. Many people get "morning wood," waking up with an erect penis. Erections can happen naturally during the night, especially during the deepest parts of sleep. Erections go away on their own or after ejaculation. As hormones even out after puberty, the number of random reflex erections decreases.

talk a lot about penis size—having a large penis is seen as better than a smaller penis. The truth is that sexual pleasure has nothing to do with penis size. Smaller penises are just as sensitive and full of nerves as bigger penises.

The penis has one hole: the urethra, which is at the very tip of the head. All the fluids that come out of a penis—pre-ejaculate (the clear liquid emitted when you're aroused), semen (the white, sticky liquid that's full of sperm), and urine—come out of the body through this hole. Ejaculation of sperm, or cumming, happens when a penis is erect. Scientists estimate that thirty-nine million sperm are in the average glob of ejaculate.

Behind the penis is the scrotum, a sack of loose skin and muscle. The scrotum and penis are sensitive to temperature and will shrink when the air is colder. Inside the sack are two testes, or balls, that vary in size from about olive-sized to about apricot-sized. Testes are where sperm

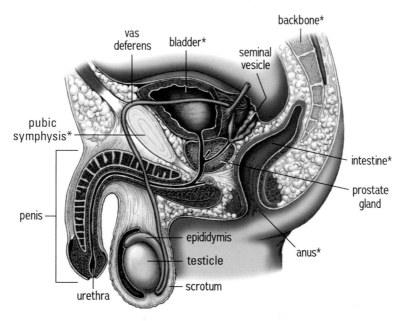

*not part of the reproductive system

is made. The testes are constantly making a tremendous amount of sperm—an average of 290 million sperm cells a day. Sperm moves out of the testes and into the penis in a little tube called the vas deferens. If sperm isn't ejaculated, it dissolves back into the body and is recycled into new sperm.

BUTTS AND BREASTS

Compared to penises and vulvas, butts are simple. Everyone has one! Butts are full of nerve endings, so they're supersensitive. The visible ring-shaped opening between your cheeks is the anus. Inside is a canal called the rectum, which some people use for anal sex. If you're ever going to insert something into your rectum, do so with extreme caution. It's easy to tear the sensitive skin around the anus. Proceed very slowly and use a water-based lubricant, which is sold at drugstores.

Everyone has nipples and breasts too. Breasts come in all shapes and sizes. Many people's breasts include glands to produce milk. Biologically, small breasts can be just as sensitive and good at producing milk as big breasts. Genetics and weight determine breast size. Typically, breasts are a slightly different size and grow at different rates. If one of your breasts is a little bigger than the other, that's normal.

Studies show that regardless of a person's gender, nipple stimulation lights up the same part of the brain as genital stimulation. But nipple sizes and sensitivities vary. Some people have supersensitive nipples, while others feel hardly anything on their nipples. Nipples get softer and harder throughout the day. They get bigger and harder when they're cold and smaller and soft when they're warm.

GENDER EXPRESSION

People present their gender in a million different ways through their clothing, hairstyles, and body posture. Psychologists usually talk about gender expression on a range between masculine and feminine. Since there are an infinite number of ways to dress and act, people are coming up with creative new ways to describe gender expression. Here are several examples:

- **Androgynous.** Someone who presents as a mix of masculine and feminine or neither, often blurring the lines between masculine and feminine. Celebrities Ruby Rose and Bex Taylor-Klaus often present androgynously.
- **Butch.** Someone who presents as masculine, usually a masculine lesbian. The term can also refer to masculine gay men or to masculine nonbinary people. Two butch celebrities are Lena Waithe and Lea DeLaria.
- **Femme.** Someone who presents as feminine. Many men who perform in drag—such as RuPaul or Trixie Mattel—aim for a femme look. The term can also refer to heterosexual women such as Beyoncé, Madonna, and Rihanna, who present femininely, or to feminine nonbinary people, such as Alok Vaid-Menan.

HOW DO YOU KNOW IF YOU'RE TRANSGENDER?

Most people have moments where they don't feel entirely like the gender they were assigned at birth. But for trans people, that feeling endures over many years. Every person's experience with gender is different—there's no one story of what it's like to be transgender. On the website Reddit, hundreds of people responded to a post asking people to recall their earliest memories of realizing they were trans, and every story was different. One trans man wrote,

> I remember as a preteen being very distressed as my chest started to grow. I hated it. Every bit of it. I was so embarrassed and disgusted by the little bumps starting to protrude under my shirts. As a teenager, I overcompensated in femininity because I felt that's what would garner me attention from people, what would make

WHO ARE YOU ANYWAY?

Biological sex is a category that includes external genitalia and internal biology, such as chromosomes and hormones. When babies are born, doctors usually label them male or female based on external anatomy. But gender identity is defined by how you think about yourself. Do you think of yourself as a boy? As a girl? As neither? Or does it change day to day?

People use many terms to describe their gender identity, and they are constantly inventing new terms. In the "Gender Nation Glossary," the Gay & Lesbian Alliance Against Defamation and the lifestyle website Refinery29 define three main gender identities that fall outside the binary:

AGENDER: a person who does not identify with any gender

GENDER FLUID: someone for whom gender identity and presentation is on a spectrum. A gender-fluid person may fluctuate between presenting as feminine, masculine, neither, or both.

NONBINARY: a person who experiences their gender identity, gender expression, or both outside the categories of man or woman

Instead of using the pronouns she/her or he/him to describe themselves, people who identify outside the binary may choose to describe themselves with gender neutral pronouns, such as they/them. For example, "I saw Em at the store today, and they were buying my favorite cheese!" The pronouns you use to define yourself are a personal decision. If people don't ask you which pronouns you prefer, let them know. And if you don't ask someone which pronouns they prefer, you may be misgendering them, which is rude and hurtful.

me liked. I wore push-up bras and just tried really hard to be something I wasn't. At 18 and 19, I started really getting into cosplay, but instead of choosing female characters, I was always gravitating towards male. It's where I felt comfortable, where I felt . . . REAL.

Many transgender people know they are trans when they are as young as four or five. For other people, it can take a long time to figure out what feels right. Some transgender or nonbinary people don't start experimenting with clothing, makeup, fashions, and haircuts to find what feels "real" until they are adults. Then some people may talk to a doctor about using hormones, surgery, or both to transition medically. This long process involves counseling and meetings with doctors.

When a person is sure about the decision to transition and has the okay from doctors, they may choose to start taking hormones. People who are transitioning to male will take testosterone, and people who are transitioning to female will take estrogen. The effects of hormones are profound, impacting everything from where hair grows on your body to the shape of your face. Some people decide to have gender-confirmation surgery such as top surgery (breast augmentation or removal) or bottom surgery (genital reconstruction surgery or removal of the ovaries, uterus, or testes).

These options require careful consideration, discussion with medical professionals, and personal research. Not everyone who is trans decides to start taking hormones or get surgery. Some trans people feel right in their bodies after changing things like their name, hair, pronouns, and clothing.

DEFINING YOUR DESIRES

It would be nice if we could decide exactly to whom we would be attracted, right? It would be convenient to not get a crush on the emotionally unavailable person who's totally wrong for you. But the heart works in mysterious ways. The term *sexual orientation* describes your inherent, enduring emotional, romantic, or sexual attraction to other people.

"Am I gay? Am I bisexual? Am I straight?" Sexual attraction is complicated! People's identities often become more complex and shift throughout their lives as they gain more experience. In the 1940s, researcher and biologist Alfred Kinsey interviewed thousands of Americans about their sex lives. His groundbreaking research showed that many people aren't entirely straight or entirely gay. Instead, human sexuality is on a spectrum. "The world is not to be divided into sheep and goats," he wrote. "The living world is a continuum in each and every one of its aspects." Based on this idea, he developed the Kinsey Scale, which ranges from one (100 percent heterosexual) to six (100 percent homosexual). An x stands for people who don't feel much sexual attraction at all. That's called asexuality. Asexual people might want to partner with someone and be emotionally romantic and intimate but without the drive to be physically intimate.

ASEXUALITY: THE INVISIBLE ORIENTATION

Some people don't feel sexual at all and don't enjoy sex. That's normal. The website *What Is Asexuality?* lists these questions to help evaluate whether you might be asexual:

- Are you generally disinterested in the idea of sex?
- Is your interest in sex more scientific than emotional?
- Have you ever had to pretend to be interested in sex to fit in?
- Have you ever felt "broken" because you don't experience sexual feelings as do those around you?
- Have you ever felt that you were straight "by default" or that you were bisexual because you were equally disinterested in all genders?
- Have you ever gone out with someone or had sex because you felt "that's what you're supposed to do?"

Many people identify somewhere in the range between 100 percent heterosexual and 100 percent homosexual. How many people in the United States identify as not entirely straight? A 2016 survey of 1.6 million Americans found that 4.1 percent of people identified as either lesbian, gay, bisexual, or transgender. That would mean roughly ten million adults in the United States identify as LGBT. Age makes a big difference in how people identify. People born after 1980 are more than twice as likely as older folks to identify as LGBT. According to a 2016 survey by the Gay & Lesbian Alliance Against Defamation, about 12 to 16 percent of young people in the United States identify as somewhere on the LGBTQ spectrum. Young adult author Juno Dawson says, "Just because LGBT people are in a minority, it doesn't mean they are not NORMAL. People with blue eyes are in the minority, but we don't think of them as abnormal, do we? We don't look at Jake Gyllenhaal and say, LOOK AT THAT MASSIVE, BLUE-EYED FREAK!"

SEXUAL ORIENTATION BY AGE (IN PERCENT)

	18–34	35–51	54–71	72+
Heterosexual	84	91	94	98
Bisexual	6	4	2	1
Asexual	4	1	2	>.5
Gay or lesbian	3	3	2	>.5
Pansexual	2	1	1	1

GENDER IDENTITY BY AGE (IN PERCENT)

	18–34	35–51	54–71	72+
Cisgender	88	94	97	97
Agender	3	>.5	>.5	1
Gender fluid	3	1	—	—
Transgender	2	1	>.5	—
Unsure or questioning	2	3	2	2
Bigender	1	>.5	1	—

"WE'RE HERE, WE'RE QUEER!"

Cultures around the world are deeply ingrained with heterosexism—discrimination and prejudice based on the idea that heterosexuality is the only "normal" sexual orientation. Heterosexism exists in US laws. For many years, it was illegal to have sex with someone of your same gender, for women to wear "men's" clothes and vice versa, and for anyone other than a straight couple to marry. American pop culture reflects heterosexism too—LGBTQ characters are in the minority on-screen—and it plays out in violent behavior as well, with LGBTQ people facing high levels of violence. Through decades of activism, acceptance of LGBTQ people has grown enormously. Some legal protections are in place too.

LGBTQ PEOPLE STILL FACE PREJUDICE AND DISCRIMINATION EVEN THOUGH SCIENTIFIC RESEARCH SHOWS THAT SEXUAL ORIENTATION IS NOT A CHOICE.

Yet LGBTQ people still face prejudice and discrimination even though scientific research shows that sexual orientation is not a choice. A 2008 Swedish study on twins concluded that "homosexual behaviour is largely shaped by genetics and random environmental factors." In recent years, anthropologists researching human sexuality have looked back through thousands of years of history trying to find universal patterns of behavior. What they've found is that humans are defined by difference. For as far back as we can see in human history, there have always been men who have sex with men, women who have sex with women, and asexual people.

IT JUST AIN'T SO

LGBTQ people face all kinds of stereotypes that just aren't true. If you run across people who make statements like these, let them know the ideas are false:

Kids need both a mother and father. Same-gender parents are actually great parents. A 2010 review of all the studies on same-sex parenting found no differences between children raised by heterosexual parents and children raised by same-sex parents.

Bisexual people are just faking. People sometimes say that bisexual people need to "choose a side"—either they're gay or straight. That's not only hurtful. It doesn't make any sense. Humans can be attracted to people of all genders.

Gay men are always "girly," and gay women are always "manly." Gay and bi people, like straight people, express their gender in all kinds of ways. There are super-feminine lesbians and super-butch lesbians. The same goes for gay men. You can't tell someone's sexual orientation by how they dress or act.

People become gay because they were abused or had bad parents. Nope. No scientifically sound study has linked sexual orientation or gender identity to parental role modeling or childhood sexual abuse.

COMING OUT

If you've done some deep thinking and come to learn that you don't identify as straight, cisgender, or both, you can decide who to tell and how. Many LGBTQ people describe coming out as a lifelong process. In each new social setting and job, LGBTQ people often have to decide whether to talk about their identities. Whether to talk to someone about your sexual orientation or gender identity depends a lot on if you feel safe to come out.

Sometimes coming out is dangerous. For example, some parents kick their LGBTQ children out of the house. That makes LGBTQ youth way more likely to be homeless than straight, cisgender youth. A 2017 report from the University of Chicago found that one in ten LGBTQ people between the ages of eighteen and twenty-five had experienced homelessness in the past year. People can also be fired from their jobs or not hired for positions because of their sexual orientation or gender identity. Twenty-three states have laws banning these types of discrimination, but most do not. One in four LGBTQ people say that they've experienced some kind of discrimination at work.

On the other hand, many LGBTQ people have great experiences coming out to loving, supportive, and helpful families, friends, and coworkers. If you do decide to come out, there's no right way to share the information. You might choose to write a letter, talk about it over the phone, or tell just a small group of friends at first.

When you come out, to whom, and how is up to you. You'll know when and what feels safe and good, so follow your own sense of what is right.

QUESTIONS TO THINK ABOUT

Either I'm going crazy or I have the weirdest breasts in the world: my right breast is bigger than my left breast! Also, I have a giant hair growing out of my left nipple. It's the grossest thing! I cut it off, but it keeps growing back! Am I just a big freak, or is there something, like, medically wrong with me and my hairy, misshapen boobs?

Breasts are funny, aren't they? While the image of breasts we see in movies and magazines are impossibly round, perfect melons, it's actually more common for breasts to be slightly different sizes than for them to be evenly symmetrical. As one doctor quipped to *Self* magazine, "They are sisters, not twins." Also, breasts fluctuate in size depending on where you are in the menstrual cycle. They tend to be slightly bigger (and more sensitive) during ovulation. As for the long hair, that's normal too! About 30 percent of women report having hair on their nipples. If it freaks you out, the best option is to carefully snip off the hair—shaving or plucking it could cause ingrown hairs.

I'm straight and my best friend came out last year as gay. I want to be supportive of them, but I'm not sure how. What can I do to be a good ally?

The first step to being a good ally for anyone of a marginalized identity is to listen. That means actually listening to your friend when they're talking about their experiences and feelings. But it also means seeking out other voices to listen to: read books about LGBTQ history and identity, follow social media accounts of proud LGBTQ folks, and watch movies that center on LGBTQ characters. These will help you understand the history and social context behind issues.

As an ally, use your position to reach out to other straight people. If you hear someone saying something homophobic, talk to them about it. Talk to your family about LGBTQ issues. Don't out your friend to anyone. Be part of building a network of support that will help protect anyone who's LGBTQ.

CHAPTER THREE
MACHO MEN AND GIRLY GIRLS

From a very young age, we get messages about how we should dress, look, and behave based on our gender. Stores often divide clothes for babies into pink girl clothes and blue boy clothes. When humanlike figurines are marketed to girls, they're called dolls. When they're marketed to boys, they're called action figures. In these ways, gender is socially constructed. Society builds and reinforces the rules.

MAN UP!

Joe Ehrmann was a linebacker for the Baltimore Colts in the National Football League. For many people, that's the epitome of the macho guy. But Ehrmann says the three scariest words a boy can hear are "Be a man." Ehrmann remembers his dad taught him that "men don't need. Men don't want. Men don't touch. Men don't feel."

Educator and antiviolence advocate Tony Porter says of men, "From a young age, we're taught not to express our emotions." Studies show the mental health benefits of talking about feelings, but boys are taught to repress their feelings so they don't appear weak. Feelings have to go somewhere. Unable to talk about feelings, adult men are three times more likely to commit suicide than women, more likely to abuse alcohol and drugs, and much less likely to seek help for mental health issues. And with few ways to express feelings through words, a man's emotions are more likely to burst out in violent and inappropriate ways such as bullying and physical violence.

Attitudes, behavior, and discrimination based on traditional stereotypes of gender roles limit how we express ourselves. And this limit has a name. It's called sexism.

SWIMMING IN SEXISM

Pop culture and media are among the most influential forces that shape values, behavior, and a person's sense of identity. The movies you watch, the photos you scroll through on Instagram, the TV you stream, and the magazines you read—all of these send messages about what's "normal" and what's not. Many of the messages are not very obvious, but they sink in deeply.

You might not notice sexism because it's all around you every day. For example,

→ **Do you feel comfortable signing up for whatever activities you want in school?** Or do you and your friends think of some activities as for "boys only" and some for "girls only"? If you're a boy, would you sign up for ballet classes? According to a study by a dance sociologist at Wayne State University in Detroit, 93 percent of boys who took ballet were bullied and harassed.

→ **Do you feel as if you can pursue any career?** Or are some jobs considered not an option for you because they're too "girly" or "manly"? Men make up 91 percent of construction workers. Women make up 97 percent of preschool teachers. What factors contribute to this gender split?

→ **Do you speak up in class?** Studies of elementary and middle school classrooms show that boys are eight times more likely than girls to call out answers. Teachers are also more likely to listen to boys than to girls. By contrast, teachers scold girls who call out answers in class, telling them to raise their hands before speaking.

The most important way to fight back against sexism is to recognize that it exists. Keep an eye out for gender-based patterns in your own life. Listen to, read about, and believe people who are hurt by discrimination. Try to change your own behavior so you don't contribute to gender stereotypes. Taking these steps is part of being a feminist. Feminism is believing in and advocating for equal rights for all people.

DEALING WITH DISCRIMINATION

Discrimination is based on core aspects of identity such as gender (sexism), race (racism), sexual orientation (homophobia), gender identity (transphobia), economic class (classism), and ability (ableism). Discrimination happens institutionally in laws, official government decisions, and public policies. It also happens culturally through individual and group behaviors. Here are some questions to ask yourself and your friends to identify institutional and cultural discrimination in your school:

- **What race and gender are the people in positions of power at your school?** Nationally, about 80 percent of teachers are white, 7 percent are black and 2 percent are Asian. The vast majority of teachers are women (77 percent). Only 52 percent of principals are women.
- **Who gets in trouble during class?** Schools are much more likely to suspend black students than students of any other race. Boys are more likely to be suspended than girls.
- **Can someone in a wheelchair get everywhere in your school?** In New York City, 83 percent of public schools are not fully accessible to people with disabilities,

often because schools don't have elevators and students have to use stairs to get to their classrooms.

Discrimination also occurs in dating and sexuality. And it's not pretty. Data from OkCupid, an online dating, friendship, and social networking site, showed that most men on the site rated black women as less attractive than women of other races and ethnicities. Women rated Asian men as less desirable than other races. On Grindr, a dating app for men seeking men, researchers found 15 percent of men included racist preferences, such as "I don't date Asians—sorry not sorry," on their profiles.

So what can you do to fight discrimination? The first step is to listen to the people who are being discriminated against. Often, when people speak up to say they have experienced some kind of discrimination, harassment, or abuse, members of the dominant group don't believe them or they try to justify the hurtful behavior. This makes it even harder to speak up.

Another step is to examine your own behavior and change your actions and your words. Do you have biases about whom you would date? Have you ever made fun of someone for their gender or sexual orientation? Changing attitudes, behaviors, and word choices isn't something you can master in a day. It builds over time, and making an effort counts for a lot.

Another important step is to speak up when you witness discrimination. Are your friends, coworkers, or family members talking about girls in a demeaning way? Did someone make a racist joke in class? Did a friend use the word *gay* as a slur? It's often scary to call out this behavior, but it makes a big difference. When you hear someone talking in a discriminatory way, you can say, "I don't like that word" or "That sounds racist to me" or "Isn't that pretty sexist?" Even if the person brushes off the criticism or laughs at your comment, they will know where you stand and they may think twice about making the same statement again. If you find that someone you know continues to say offensive things in front of you, try to avoid them or pull yourself out of the conversation altogether. Sometimes staying away from prejudiced people is the best move.

EMOTIONAL LABOR

Talking about feelings is complicated by gender dynamics in society that instill the idea that "real men" don't talk about their emotions. Men are too often taught that a core part of masculinity is to never cry or express sadness but to instead bottle up feelings and act "tough." One impact of this situation is that men are more likely to repress their emotions only to have them explode in violent, destructive ways. And then women end up carrying the burden of talking about feelings. Having to manage the emotions and expectations of others and do the heavy lifting of taking care of someone else's feelings is emotional labor.

> HAVING TO MANAGE THE EMOTIONS AND EXPECTATIONS OF OTHERS . . . IS EMOTIONAL LABOR.

Examples of emotional labor include organizing social events, being a good host by making sure everyone feels welcome and included, feeding friends and family, pitching in to clean without being asked, recognizing when someone is upset and helping them out, and talking people through tough times. Emotional labor isn't bad— you're lucky if you have someone in your life who is skilled in these social tasks. But emotional labor needs to be recognized and appreciated.

In an article in *Harper's Bazaar,* author Gemma Hartley gives a clear example of the emotional labor division in her household: "My son will boast of his clean room and any other jobs he has done; my daughter will quietly put her clothes in the hamper and get dressed each day without being asked. They are six and four respectively. Unless I engage in this conversation on emotional labor and actively change the roles we inhabit, our children will do the same. . . . Our sons can still learn to carry their own weight. Our daughter can learn to not carry others'."

In your relationships, keep an eye on who buys presents, makes dinner, cleans up, organizes events, and brings up the difficult-to-discuss issues. Regardless of gender, everyone should appreciate the emotional labor that goes into life and work hard to speak honestly about their feelings.

THE PRINCESS PROBLEM

In the 1989 Disney classic *The Little Mermaid,* mermaid princess Ariel is designed to be a very specific ideal of feminine beauty. She has big blue eyes, large breasts, a tiny waist, and completely smooth wrinkle-and-freckle-free white skin. Ariel's body is so out of proportion with reality that her eyes are actually bigger than her waist! Pop culture researcher Sarah Coyne looked at the effect Disney princesses have on body image. She found that girls who consumed most princess-themed pop culture over time had the lowest body esteem: "Disney Princesses represent some of the first examples of exposure to the thin ideal. As women, we get it our whole lives, and it really does start at the Disney Princess level, at age three and four," she said.

And it's not just Disney. A University of South Florida analysis of American children's movies reported that 72 percent of these films "associated thinness with positive character traits such as kindness, and three out of four equated obesity with undesirable qualities." These images affect real kids. For example, by age ten, 80 percent of American girls say they've been on a diet. In a survey by the British youth organization Girlguiding, 66 percent of girls ages seventeen to twenty-one said they felt they were "not pretty enough" most of the time, and 61 percent felt they "need to be perfect" most of the time.

Think back to the movies you grew up watching and are watching now. Can you think of positive female characters who are fat or small-chested? How many positive male characters can you think of who are physically small or not strong? How many positive characters can you think of who have dark skin? How many are gay, bi, lesbian, or trans?

DOES IT PASS THE BECHDEL TEST?

Frustrated by male-dominated movies, cartoonist Alison Bechdel once jokingly suggested rating films by whether they include women. The idea took off. To pass the Bechdel Test, films must have three things:

- At least two women characters with names have roles.
- They talk to each other.
- They talk about something besides a man.

The Bechdel Test isn't about determining whether a movie is good or bad. It's a helpful tool for critically considering the roles women play on-screen. Make a list with a friend of movies you've seen lately. Do you think they pass or fail the Bechdel Test?

WHO GETS TO SPEAK?

In 2016 the University of Southern California Annenberg School for Communication and Journalism released a study of 4,554 speaking characters in nine hundred American films released since 2007. The study found that 71 percent of the actors were white. Of those thousands of characters, only 67 were gay male characters, 20 were lesbian characters, 16 were bisexual characters, and 1 was a transgender character.

RACE MATTERS

In the real world, people of all races fall in love, have relationships, and build lives together. But on-screen, almost all the main characters are white. In 2015 only 25 percent of speaking roles in movies went to people of color. When nonwhite characters do show up, they often play the roles of villains or criminals.

Stories impact how we see ourselves, how we see other people, and what we think of as normal. One 2012 study, by the University of Michigan and Indiana University, found that white boys felt good about themselves after watching TV. Girls and boys of color, meanwhile, reported lower self-esteem as they watched TV. If you don't see people like you represented in a positive way in the media, it can make you feel that there's something wrong with the way you are.

Be a critical consumer. Think about the messages movies and TV are sending. Know that regardless of what you see on-screen, you are always the hero of your own story.

SELLING BEAUTY

Do you ever feel as if there's something wrong with the way your body looks? Studies show that American men and women are significantly more unhappy with their bodies than people outside the United States. In other nations around the world, 88 percent of women and 90 percent of men say they have a positive body image. But in the United States, only 71 percent of men and 51 percent of women say they feel good about their bodies. Why do Americans feel this way? Well, because body shame is baked into our culture through movies, TV, magazines, websites, and advertising.

WHO DO YOU SEE ON-SCREEN?

How do you think the characters we see on-screen affect our image of the real world? How do film and TV shape what we think of as normal? A study by USC's Annenberg School found that

- 66.5 percent of speaking roles in films and TV are male characters;
- 34 percent of female characters on-screen wear sexy clothing;
- 8 percent of male characters on-screen wear sexy clothing;
- 89 percent of nurses in films are female;
- 10 percent of doctors in films are female;
- 5 percent of presidents in films are female;
- 28 percent of speaking characters in film and TV are people of color;
- 6.4 percent of characters on prime-time TV shows are LGBTQ; and
- 1.8 percent of characters on prime-time TV shows have a disability.

When you open a magazine or scroll through ads on Instagram, the models you see are almost certainly photoshopped to have wrinkles removed, skin smoothed and lightened, and limbs slimmed down. Most of the glowing faces you see in ads are genuinely humanly impossible. But that doesn't stop us from comparing ourselves to the impossible. In 2018 one poll of one thousand Americans discovered that 83 percent of women and 74 percent of men said they felt dissatisfied with how their bodies looked—often while comparing themselves to both friends and celebrities they see on social media.

For example, the average American woman is 5 feet 4 (1.6 m) and weighs 140 pounds (63 kg). But the average American model is 5 feet 11 (1.8 m) and weighs 117 pounds (53 kg). Among girls between the ages of six and twelve, 40 to 60 percent are concerned about their weight or about becoming too fat. In high school, the skinny-is-best ideal persists.

No one wakes up one morning and decides they're inadequate. According to behaviorist and sex educator Emily Nagoski, the idea "sneaks in under the fence and invades like poison ivy." She says that the message many people—especially women—get from pop culture about their bodies and sexuality is, "You are inadequate." She points out that when we look at the bodies and stories featured in media, they send a clear message: "You're too fat and too thin; your breasts are too big and too small. Your body is wrong. If you're not trying to change it, you're lazy. If you're satisfied with yourself as you are, you're settling. And if you dare to actively like yourself, you're a conceited bitch! In short, you are doing it wrong. Do it differently. No, that's wrong, too, try something else. Forever." Nagoski also says that "women have cultural permission to criticize ourselves, but we are punished if we praise ourselves, if we dare to like ourselves the way we are."

Why does this toxic dynamic persist? Partly because corporations make a lot of money by convincing people that every inch of their bodies needs to be fixed. In the United States alone, the diet industry makes $68.2 billion a year. In 2017 the global skin-care market was

FIGHT BACK AGAINST BODY SHAME

1. NIX THE NEGGING. "I look so fat." "Her butt is huge!" "He's such a whale." These are small remarks that are super hurtful. Make sure you're not contributing to a culture of body shaming by cutting down yourself or others.

2. CELEBRATE WHAT'S REAL. Try not to compare yourself and your friends to the impossible bodies of celebrities. Instead, make yourself and your friends feel good. Does your best friend have a good sense of style? A wonderful laugh? Tell them! And don't forget to look for positive things to tell yourself too.

3. OPEN UP. If you are feeling negative about your body, find someone—a friend, sibling, parent, or counselor—to talk to about it. Getting the feelings off your chest and reframing them with help from another person is part of saying no to body shaming. It's a good way to take care of your emotional health too.

4. LISTEN. If someone comes to you to talk about their body shame, listen without offering advice. Don't suggest a diet or a new workout. Compassionate listening is one of the best things you can offer.

worth $128 billion. That includes everything from anti-acne pads to lotions that promise to end aging and creams that aim to make dark skin lighter. So be a critically thinking consumer. Ask yourself, Why do I think I need this product? Can I spend my money in a way that builds on what I love about myself?

FAT IS FINE!

Media and pop culture usually equate being skinny with being healthy. The reality is that you can't tell if someone is healthy just by looking at them. Human bodies come in all shapes and sizes. Studies show that what makes someone healthy or unhealthy isn't their weight. It's their lifestyle choices. "Fat but fit" people who exercise regularly, eat plenty of fresh fruits and vegetables, and who don't smoke have no higher risk of death or illness than people with the same habits who weigh less. Skinny people aren't necessarily healthier. Thin people can still get diabetes, heart disease, or heart attacks.

One medically reliable sign of health is your metabolism. Metabolism is the internal process by which your body converts the food you've eaten into energy and burns calories. How fast your metabolism works is determined mostly by genetics, so people can have a fast, slow, or average metabolism regardless of their size. Getting enough exercise is key to having a healthy metabolism. Doctors recommend thirty minutes of movement (walking, dancing, skateboarding, biking, anything!) a day. What makes someone healthy is linked to what they eat and whether they exercise—not what their body looks like.

FOOD FIGHTS

Many teenagers, regardless of gender, feel intense pressure to look a certain way, usually thin and buff. Many develop eating disorders. Disordered eating can range from relatively mild conditions such as skipping a meal sometimes, even if you're hungry, because you're trying to lose weight. It can also be a really serious condition such as starving yourself (anorexia), forcing yourself to throw up (bulimia), or a pattern of stuffing yourself with a ton of food all in one go (binge eating). Some people have more than one eating disorder. Disordered eating affects about 2.7 percent of American teens, or just over 1.1 million people. Eating disorders aren't just about food and body size—they're a treatable mental illness. Low self-esteem, depression, and anxiety all contribute to eating disorders. So do external stressors such as pressure to get perfect grades or snag a specific job.

What does it feel like to have an eating disorder? *Riverdale* star Camila Mendes talked openly about having an eating disorder as a teenager. "I was so scared of carbs that I wouldn't let myself eat bread or rice ever. I'd go a week without eating them, then I would binge on them, and that would make me want to purge," Mendes said. "I was consumed with the details of what I was eating, and I always felt as if I was doing something wrong." At the age of twenty-three, Mendes started seeing a therapist who has helped her manage her stress and stop her self-destructive eating behaviors. "The voices in my head never completely go away. They're just way quieter now," she said.

If you or someone you know has an eating disorder, help is out there. Talk to a counselor, a parent, a doctor, or someone else you trust. If left untreated, eating disorders can be deadly. Every sixty-two minutes, someone in the United States dies as a direct result of having an eating disorder, often from heart attacks, starvation, and suicide. Seeking help is not a weakness or a failure. It's just the opposite—it's an act of bravery and self-love.

SELF-CARE IS ESSENTIAL

Taking steps to appreciate and celebrate your body is actually a pretty radical act. Self-care isn't just doing nice things for yourself, like eating chocolate or taking a warm bath. It's checking in to make sure you're taking care of yourself—mentally, physically, and spiritually. Here are ways to practice self-care in a positive way:

EXERCISE FOR FUN. Being physically active in any way releases chemicals in the brain called endorphins that make us feel good. You don't need to be running marathons or hitting a million home runs to get the benefits of endorphins and to be strong and healthy. Find an activity or two that just makes you feel good. Dancing? Biking? Walking? Playing soccer with friends? All of those are great ways to take care of your body—and your emotional health. The benefits from the brain chemicals that exercising releases to make us feel happy and strong last over time.

TAKE A BREAK FROM YOUR PHONE. The average American adult spends more than ten hours a day consuming media on devices.

- five hours watching TV
- two hours looking at phones or tablets

- one hour looking at the internet on a computer
- fifteen minutes playing video games

A 2016 survey of young adults by the National Institute of Mental Health in the United States found that the more time a person spends looking at social media, the more likely they are to be depressed.

How much time do you spend a day consuming media? Try keeping a log for a week to track the time you spend watching TV, looking at a phone or tablet, watching films or TV shows on a computer, playing video games, and listening to the radio. You'll be surprised at the results.

Do yourself a favor. Put your phone down for a while. Try to do so for a few minutes every day and gradually build up the time. And get some face time instead. Talk to a friend in person, take a walk with your favorite neighbor, or read a book aloud with someone you like. You'll feel better about yourself, and the people in your life will love it too.

WRITE DOWN TEN THINGS YOU LIKE ABOUT YOURSELF. It's nice to have a list to look at when self-hatred and self-doubt start to creep up on you. What are ten positive things about you as a whole person besides your looks? Maybe you're generous, a good brother, a voracious reader, or a good listener. Maybe you make a mean chocolate chip cookie or you're a terrific mimic. Make a list, and add to it as you think of more things so your list keeps growing.

QUESTIONS TO THINK ABOUT

There's a guy in my class who dresses like kind of weirdly, he wears skinny jeans and pink shirts and so people call him "faggot" all the time. What should I do? They're just joking and I don't want to make it worse by making a big deal out of it, but also I feel bad for not doing anything.

You're right that although these guys say they're joking, using homophobic slurs is really hurtful. Make sure you're not encouraging any of this bad behavior. Are you laughing along? You can be a role model in your behavior. Try to treat the guy who's being bullied as if you would anyone else—with respect, generosity, and kindness.

Then speak up. You're in a relatively safe place to call out bad behavior, unlike the bullied guy in your class who might be beaten up if he talks back. When a friend uses *gay* or *faggot* as a slur, it's your responsibility to say something. Try, "I hate when people say gay is a bad thing. It's fine to be gay." Speaking up may feel awkward at first. But even if people brush you off or say you're overreacting, you've made them think twice. You're also letting people who are listening know that you're not okay with that kind of hatred and that you will stand up against it.

> I don't know how to flirt with girls without being sexist. Can I tell a girl she's beautiful, or is that like offensive?

Compliments feel awesome, but only when they're welcome, and that depends on your relationship. It's generally a bit creepy and off-putting to have a stranger or random classmate talk about your body in any way, even if it's positive. The best way to flirt with someone is to show interest in them and get to know them. If you like a girl, ask her questions. Ask her what she's into, how her weekend was, or what her opinion is about a popular movie or book. Get to know her as a full person. Save the body-specific compliments (you're gorgeous) for someone with whom you have an established romantic relationship.

CHAPTER FOUR
TAKE CARE DOWN THERE

Human bodies never stop changing. When we're babies, we grow and change quickly. Even in our thirties, forties, fifties, and beyond, the human body is always shifting. Our skin gets wrinkles, and our hormones change. Even the places where fat is on our bodies shifts around!

During puberty, body changes are intense. Most people start puberty somewhere between the ages of eight and fourteen and finish in their early twenties. Puberty happens naturally when the brain releases the gonadotropin-releasing hormone into the bloodstream. That one hormone kicks off a whole bunch of changes.

Hormones affect everyone in different ways, so the way your friends' bodies change during puberty won't be exactly the way yours changes. Here are the major changes that happen during puberty:

Getting taller. During puberty, you'll go through a series of growth spurts and eventually reach your full adult height. Height is determined by genetics, so you can't make yourself taller or shorter.

Body hair. Whatever your gender, you'll see hair grow on your armpits, legs, face, stomach, back, chest, and pubic region. Your hairiness depends on your hormones and your genetics. What you do about the hair is up to you. Wherever it's growing, it's totally fine to leave it alone. If you decide to shave it off, be careful! Shaving can cause painful ingrown hairs and razor burn, and it's easy to cut yourself. Use hot water (to open pores), shaving cream, a sharp razor, and lotion afterward to minimize the negative impacts shaving has on skin. Girls and women are under more pressure to remove their body hair. An American woman spends, on average, $10,000 over her lifetime on body hair removal.

Zits. When hormones change, many teens start getting pimples on their face, back, and chest. A bunch of things cause pimples: hormones, dead skin and oil that clog pores, and diets that include a lot of dairy and sugars. For clearer skin, try to reduce stress, eat healthy foods, and wash with a salicylic acid-based soap three to five mornings a week. Avoid picking and popping pimples since that can cause scars.

Smelly armpits. The hormonal changes in your body cause sweating and body odor. Try a couple of deodorant options, and see what works best for you.

Mood swings. The hormones running through your body can make your moods more intense. People going through puberty often experience a lot of emotional ups and downs. If you're feeling extra irritable, sad, or emotional, find outlets for your feelings. Talk to a friend or trusted adult, or write your thoughts regularly in a journal. Bottling up emotions only makes things worse.

If you have testes, you'll probably experience the following:

→ **Testicle and penis growth.** Typically, the first change in puberty is that the skin of the scrotum becomes thinner and the testicles hang lower. The penis also begins to get bigger. Penises come in all sizes. A bigger penis is not better than a smaller penis.

→ **Upper–body muscle growth.** Chest muscles (pectorals) and shoulder muscles (deltoids) start to flesh out. If you do decide to lift weights or do other exercises to tone your growing muscles, be careful to take it slow to avoid injury.

→ **Voice deepening.** Everyone has vocal cords, the two muscles that stretch kind of like rubber bands across the larynx, a hollow organ in the throat. The sound of your voice is made by the vibration of the vocal cords. During puberty, the larynx gets bigger and the vocal cords lengthen and thicken, so your voice gets deeper. Your voice might crack occasionally, but that phase doesn't last for long.

→ **Tender nipples.** You might notice swelling and tenderness underneath your breasts. Hormones cause this. This swelling is normal and almost always gone by the age of twenty.

If you have ovaries, you'll probably experience the following:

→ **Curves.** You'll notice your body changing shape. Your hips and butt will get curvier, and your body will likely flesh out overall. This is healthy. It's unhealthy to diet while your body is going through puberty. Being undernourished can cause serious problems such as weak bones for the rest of your life. Embrace the curves!

→ **Breast growth.** Your breasts will grow—sometimes a little, sometimes a lot! Breasts of all sizes are wonderful.

No exercises or magic supplements will make your
breasts bigger or smaller.

→ Menstruation. When you notice red or brown stains
in your underwear, you've started menstruating. People
with ovaries typically get their period two years after
their breasts start to grow.

SO WHAT IS MENSTRUATION, ANYWAY?

Period, shark week, that time of the month. The hormonal cycle that
creates menstruation impacts the body not just for one week out of
every month but all the time. (The word *menstruation* comes from
menses, the plural of *mensis,* which means "month" in Latin.) For people
with ovaries, the brain releases hormones that impact emotions, fertility,
sexual desire, and other aspects of physical health. The impact of those
hormones changes during about twenty-eight days, and the cycle
repeats over and over for decades.

Cycles usually take years to become regular. Usually, when people
first get their period, they might miss their period every once in a while or
the time between periods may vary. Lots of things—stress, diet, exercise,
and anything else that can throw hormones out of whack—affects how
much you bleed, how long you bleed, and even if you bleed.

Not everyone with a uterus gets a period. About 3 percent of people
with ovaries don't start getting a period when they go through puberty.
That's called amenorrhea. If someone starts having a period and then
it stops for six months or longer, that's called secondary amenorrhea.
Extreme exercising, disordered eating, endocrine problems, or chronic
illnesses such as diabetes, Crohn's disease, or ovarian cysts can cause
amenorrhea. See your doctor if you experience any of these conditions.

When they are adults, some transgender and nonbinary people take
the hormone testosterone or have a hysterectomy surgery to remove
the uterus. These steps end the menstrual cycle permanently. For
everyone with a uterus, the menstrual cycle eventually ends with age.

Typically, between the ages of forty-eight to fifty-five, people go through menopause. The ovaries start producing less of the hormones estrogen and progesterone, and the menstrual cycle ceases.

The menstrual cycle follows a pattern. At the beginning of the cycle, the pituitary gland in the brain releases hormones that cause an egg in the ovaries to mature and release. The egg moves through the fallopian tubes to the uterus. As the egg is maturing and making its way down the fallopian tubes, the uterus prepares for its arrival. This part of the cycle is ovulation. The uterus builds up its interior lining—the endometrium—to give the egg a cozy, nourishing place to land. If sperm fertilizes the egg, the egg will attach to the uterine lining and start to grow. This is the very beginning of pregnancy.

If sperm is not around to fertilize the egg, it remains unfertilized. Then the uterus sheds its extra-thick lining. That lining flows out of

GET SOME SLEEP!

Are you a night owl? You're not the only one! Hormones tell us when we're sleepy and when we're awake. When these hormones change during puberty, our internal clock shifts. High school and college students are naturally awake later at night than younger kids and older adults. Studies show that teenagers truly do have a different sense of time. The time teens naturally fall asleep gets later and later, reaching its latest point by the age of twenty. After that, it gradually gets earlier again. By the age of fifty-five, research shows, you naturally wake about the same time as you did when you were ten.

Research also shows that the teen brain works better if a person can start the school day at 10 a.m. or later. So if yours starts super early and you're going to bed super late, you might find yourself falling asleep in class. If so, adjust the time you go to bed so you get at least a full eight hours of sleep every night.

the uterus through the cervix (at the top of the vaginal canal) and then through the vagina and out of the body. The flow lasts two to seven days. Getting your period is a sure sign you are not pregnant. Periods start in puberty about two to three years after the breasts start growing. The average age for starting a period is twelve or thirteen. People feel all sorts of ways about getting their period. Some people are excited to be getting older. Other people are scared, confused, and surprised. There's no right way to react.

IS THAT . . . BLOOD?!?

Menstrual flow is often described as blood because it's a reddish-brown fluid. But it's actually only about 35 percent blood. The rest of the fluid is uterine lining, which often has little clumps of cells and blobs of mucus in it.

The amount of fluid that comes out of the body during a period varies for everyone and often fluctuates every month. While it might seem like a lot of fluid, periods usually have less fluid than 1/2 cup (118 mL) of water. An average light flow would be just 1 tablespoon (15 mL) of fluid over the course of the week. A heavy flow is about 6 tablespoons (90 mL). Some people have periods that are really light, never getting much fluid and just spotting of red and brown discharge. Other people have extremely heavy periods, soaking more than one pad or tampon an hour. Both of these conditions can be an indication of something unhealthy going on in your body, so talk with a doctor about this.

PERIOD PROBLEMS

You're watching a corny movie on TV, but you can't stop yourself from tearing up. And your lower belly hurts. When your dad asks what's wrong, you snap at him.

Moodiness, cramps, and crying spells are all symptoms of premenstrual syndrome, better known as PMS. In the days before each period, at least 75 percent of menstruators experience PMS.

The menstrual cycle causes fluctuations in brain chemistry and hormones that create a range of symptoms such as cramps, mood swings, feeling sensitive or depressed, and breast sensitivity. Other symptoms include headaches, acne flare-ups, constipation, fatigue, joint pain, bloating, and joint pain.

Some people have cramps that are so painful, they're debilitating. Periods should not leave you regularly bedridden. If it's hard to go about your regular life when you have your period—the pain is so bad that it's tough to get out of bed, go to school, focus in class, and play sports—see your doctor. Two common conditions that cause terrible menstrual cramps are cysts and endometriosis. Endometriosis is a painful disorder in which tissue that normally lines the inside of your uterus—the endometrium—grows outside your uterus. Ovarian or uterine cysts are growths that can cause pelvic pain and pain while peeing or pooping. Both can be treated, so talk to a doctor.

Hormonal birth control methods such as the Pill, intrauterine devices (IUDs), and vaginal rings often help ease the symptoms of PMS. They

DEALING WITH PMS

Many people take over-the-counter medications to help with PMS. You can also try these natural remedies:

5. Use heat to reduce cramps. Taking a hot bath or putting a heating pad or hot water bottle on your lower belly can ease muscle pain and cramping.

6. Exercise. Physical activity, even a short walk, helps fight mood swings and fatigue.

7. Take calcium. Research shows that menstruating people who take two calcium supplements a day have less period-related depression and fatigue.

8. Eat ginger. Studies show that consuming ginger reduces nausea, headaches, and muscle pains caused by PMS. Try ginger tea or add grated fresh ginger to your favorite stir-fry

reduce cramps, prevent menstrual-related migraine headaches, help control endometriosis and uterine cysts, and improve acne. Actually, 33 percent of teens get a prescription from their doctor to take the Pill to manage their period and its side effects.

You're in charge of your body. Keep track of what's going on with your hormonal changes and your genitalia. Get to know what's normal for you so you can be the best expert about how to take care of and advocate for you.

QUESTIONS TO THINK ABOUT

I feel as if I missed something. I'm thirteen and I haven't gotten my period or had my breasts get bigger or gotten much taller at all. All my friends talk about having to shave their armpits and buy tampons, and I nod along as if I know what they're talking about. Is there something wrong with me?

If you haven't started puberty by the time you're thirteen or fourteen, you might be among the 3 percent of Americans who experience delayed puberty. About 90 percent of the time when puberty is delayed, doctors will take a "wait and watch" approach, and puberty will eventually start up naturally.

Delayed puberty can be caused by chronic illnesses such as diabetes or celiac disease. Bodies also naturally delay puberty if they don't have enough body fat, which is often seen in people who are anorexic. Check with a doctor if you think your puberty is delayed. They can do a blood test to see if something is causing the delay or if you're just naturally developing a bit later.

I'm in seventh grade, and I think I must be the only girl in school who doesn't shave her legs.

Some kids call me "mountain woman" and a lesbian. I know I could shave, but it just seems, like, not right to me. I've tried it before, and it doesn't feel good. Do all girls shave their legs? If I don't, does it mean I'm a lesbian?

Nope and nope. Women of all sexual orientations decide to remove their leg hair, armpit hair, pubic hair, and facial hair . . . or not! People who call you names or make assumptions about your sexual identity because you don't shave your legs are being ignorant and unkind. The only reason to shave your legs is if you think it looks good and feels good. No one has the right to shame and harass you into making you treat your body in a way you don't want to. Do what feels right to you.

CHAPTER FIVE
KNOW YOUR GERMS

People often get awkward when talking about sex and bodies, and that can keep them—especially young people!—from speaking up and seeking help when their reproductive and sexual organs don't feel right. Knowledge is power. You're the expert on what feels right with your body. If you're experiencing pain, burning, or any other unusual or uncomfortable physical feelings, that's a red flag to talk to a doctor. Here are some common things to watch out for:

KEEP IT CLEAN

Did you know your genitalia is home to a lot of bacteria? That's a good thing! Our bodies are home to millions of helpful bacteria that keep us working well. Every part of the body—your mouth, stomach, intestines, and genitalia—have bacteria. So just as with any other part of your body, keep your private bits clean. Genitals do a great job of self-cleaning, so don't douse them in soap. It will kill off the good bacteria that occur naturally. Instead, clean your genitalia just with warm water.

If you have a vulva, never use a douche. A douche is water or a chemical squirted into the vagina. Companies sell douches by marketing the false idea that vaginas are smelly and dirty and need to be cleaned. Actually, the opposite is true. Douches wipe out a vulva's natural, healthy bacteria, leaving it vulnerable to unhealthy, foreign bacteria. That can cause infections. So douches are a dangerous scam.

If you have a penis that's uncircumcised, the foreskin can get inflamed or infected. If your penis hurts or it stings when you pee, it may be infected. To prevent that, clean underneath the foreskin with warm water when you take a shower. Without regular cleaning, smegma, a whitish-yellow substance, can build up under the foreskin. Smegma can look like pus, but it's dead skin cells, oils, and other fluids that build up.

UTI OMG

One of the most common and painful problems for people of all genders are urinary tract infections (UTIs). A UTI occurs when bacteria that aren't normally in the bladder get inside the urethra and begin to multiply in the bladder. Bodies are designed to keep out invading bacteria. But sometimes bacteria get inside anyway.

Signs of urinary tract infections are a semi-constant tickling urge to pee, pain while peeing, peeing often in small amounts, and cloudy urine that smells bad. If you have any of these symptoms, see a doctor. If left untreated, UTIs can spread from a minor annoyance to a full-blown kidney infection. Antibiotics or natural remedies can treat UTIs. See your doctor for advice and treatment ASAP if you suspect you have a UTI.

People with vulvas are at a higher risk for UTIs because the urethra is close to the vaginal opening. Sometimes sexual activity can bring bacteria from the vagina into the urinary opening, causing a urinary tract infection. Peeing after sex reduces the risk of UTIs, so doctors will often recommend that people with vulvas go to the bathroom within fifteen minutes of vaginal intercourse.

THE YEAST OF YOUR PROBLEMS

Yeast infections are another common condition that happens to 75 percent of people with vulvas. They're not fun. A yeast infection comes with vaginal itching, swelling around the vagina, soreness, and pain during vaginal sex.

A healthy vagina contains bacteria and some yeast cells. But when the balance of bacteria and yeast changes, the yeast cells can multiply. Anything that helps bacteria grow out of control can cause yeast infections. To reduce the risk of yeast infections, do the following:

- Towel off really well after showering. Completely dry your groin.
- Don't use scented tampons or pads.
- Wear breathable cotton underwear (and pants, tights, and leggings that aren't too tight!).
- Change your tampons or menstrual pad at least every four hours.

If you think you might have a yeast infection, see your doctor for a diagnosis and treatment. Over-the-counter medications, available to people of all ages, will usually do the trick.

KISSING PROBLEMS

If you want to kiss someone, be aware of two kissing-related diseases. The first is oral herpes, a.k.a. cold sores. Herpes lives in the bloodstream of half of all Americans. Many people with this virus never have any symptoms. Most people (90 percent!) who have the oral herpes virus don't even know it. For other people, the virus will cause sores around the mouth. Some people get sores every few months, usually when they're stressed out, sick, tired, or about to get their period. The sores are clusters of little blisters that scab over. Cold sores go away on their own after about a week.

Cold sores hurt! And they're contagious. Herpes is spread by direct skin-to-skin contact between a cold sore and someone else's mouth or genitalia. You can't get herpes from sharing silverware, cups, or pillows with someone who has a cold sore. If you have oral herpes, see your doctor for a prescription antiviral medication that clears up cold sores quickly and reduces the frequency of outbreaks. Over-the-counter and prescription creams help cold sores heal faster. Long story short: If you have a cold sore, don't kiss anyone on the mouth or put your mouth on their genitals.

The other disease to know about is mononucleosis, or mono. Mono is a virus that is transmitted through saliva. You can get it through kissing but also through saliva droplets in the air from sneezing or coughing. You can also get it from sharing drinks or utensils with someone who has mono. If you have mono, you'll likely have a fever, a sore throat, and fatigue. If you have these symptoms, see a doctor. The clinic can test to see if you have mono and tell you how to deal with it. If you have mono, cover your coughs and sneezes and don't kiss anyone until the virus has gone away. There's no quick cure for mononucleosis. You have to wait, rest, and take care of yourself (often for weeks) while the body fights the infection.

SEXUALLY TRANSMITTED INFECTIONS (STIS)

STIs are infections that spread through sexual contact—any combination of contact between a mouth, vulva, penis, or anus. Before you are sexually intimate with another person, talk about your sexual histories and the risk of STIs. The best ways to prevent STIs are
- not having sex at all,
- using condoms during sex, and
- having sex that doesn't involve genital-to-genital or mouth-to-genital contact.

To prevent the spread of STIs, it's absolutely essential to know whether you have any! A lot of STIs have few or no symptoms but are still contagious, so get tested! If you're sexually active, get tested for STIs at least once a year. If you have several partners, get tested more often. Any doctor's office can test for STIs, and many cities in the United States have public health clinics that will test for free or at low cost. Because they're part of your medical record, all STI tests are always 100 percent confidential. It is against the law for a doctor or any other medical staff to share the results with your family, employer, or the public.

Many people don't get tested for STIs because they're embarrassed. But STIs are very common. Half of sexually active people in the United States will have an STI by the age of twenty-five. These are the six most common STIs in the United States:

HUMAN PAPILLOMAVIRUS (HPV)

HPV is the most common STI. Researchers estimate that at least 80 percent of sexually active Americans will have an HPV infection during their lifetime. Most of the forty known strains of HPV have no symptoms. The body gets rid of them without your ever knowing about it. Some strains of HPV cause genital warts, and others cause infections in the mouth and throat. The most dangerous strains cause a variety of cancers, including cancers of the cervix, vulva, vagina, penis, or anus. HPV vaccines protect against HPV strains that cause cervical cancer and genital warts. The Centers for Disease Control and Prevention recommends young women aged eleven to twenty-six and young men aged eleven to twenty-one get vaccinated.

CHLAMYDIA

Chlamydia is the most commonly reported STI. Bacteria causes this infection, which is treated with antibiotics. Most people have no symptoms. Some people notice an unusual discharge from the vagina or penis or pain or burning when they pee. You're contagious even if you don't have symptoms. In 2015 rates of chlamydia, gonorrhea, and syphilis reached a record high. Researchers aren't sure why, but they think it could be because fewer people are using condoms during vaginal and anal sex. If left untreated, chlamydia can lead to pelvic inflammation in women and difficulty getting pregnant.

GONORRHEA

Gonorrhea, also known as the clap, has similar symptoms to chlamydia. Most people have none. Some people experience unusual discharge and pain or burning when they pee. A doctor will prescribe antibiotics if you have this STI. If left untreated, gonorrhea can lead to long-term pain and a host of fertility problems.

SYPHILIS

At first, the main symptom of syphilis is a sore at the original site of infection. Then it turns into a rash, followed by more sores on the mouth, vulva, or anus. Left untreated, syphilis causes organ, nerve, and brain damage. In extreme cases, it can also cause death. Be sure to see a doctor if you suspect you have this STI. It can be treated with antibiotics.

GENITAL HERPES

Genital herpes is a strain of the herpes virus that causes sores on the penis, vulva, or anus. It can be spread by any genital-to-genital or mouth-to-genital contact if one of the sexual partners has a herpes sore. Genital herpes outbreaks can be suppressed by one of several antibiotics. Studies have shown that antibiotics can also reduce the number of outbreaks by at least 75 percent if the medication is taken regularly. Be sure to check with a doctor if you think you have genital herpes. And remember that if you have oral herpes, you do not automatically have genital herpes and vice versa.

HIV/AIDS

Human immunodeficiency virus (HIV) is the virus that causes acquired immunodeficiency syndrome (AIDS). The virus attacks and weakens the immune system. People with AIDS are extremely susceptible to common diseases such as the flu and pneumonia that a healthy immune system would fight off. These common illnesses are life-threatening to someone with AIDS because their body can't fight them off. Untreated, people with HIV/AIDS die from usually nonfatal illnesses such as pneumonia and the flu.

HIV is spread through body fluids, including blood, semen, vaginal fluids, and breast milk. That means you can't get HIV from kissing, hugging, sitting on a toilet seat, or sharing drinks or silverware with a person who has HIV.

You can get HIV by having unprotected vaginal or anal sex with an infected person. You can also get HIV by sharing a needle with someone who is infected. Infected mothers can pass the virus to their newborns during vaginal delivery and through breast milk.

Anyone can get HIV regardless of race or sexual orientation. In the United States, the group most at risk of contracting HIV are African American men who have sex with other men. Dennis Sifris, MD, and journalist James Myhre said, "While some may suggest that culture and sexual behavior are solely to blame for this, the fault lies more with the social and economic inequities that can fuel any infectious disease outbreak. Poverty, social injustice, and the lack of an effective government response together enable the spread of disease in communities that simply haven't the resources to combat it."

There's no cure for HIV yet, although drugs can help people with HIV live long lives. Pre-exposure antiviral medication is available for HIV-negative people to take to prevent contracting the disease. The rate of HIV infection in the United States is declining through condom use and virus-suppressing drugs. However, thousands of people every year contract HIV in the United States. Since the epidemic was identified in the early 1980s, more than 1.2 million people in the United States have received an AIDS diagnosis. Among people aged thirteen to twenty-four with HIV, an estimated 51 percent didn't know they had the disease. So get tested!

QUESTIONS TO THINK ABOUT

Does wearing tight jean shorts cause yeast infections?

Wearing tight, non-breathable fabric doesn't *cause* yeast infections, but it does make them more likely. Tight jeans, leggings, leotards, or spandex don't allow much airflow into your crotch, so your sweat builds up and makes the place warm and moist—which bacteria love. Get out of wet clothes (like workout gear or swimsuits) as soon as possible and towel off well. If you do need to wear tight clothes, give your crotch some time afterward to air out. Some doctors recommend sleeping without underwear a few nights a week.

I want to get tested for chlamydia, but I don't want to go to my family's doctor. Is there somewhere else I can go?

The Centers for Disease Control and Prevention has a website to help people find clinics that do STI testing in their area: https://gettested.cdc.gov/. Check it out! Many clinics do STI tests for free or at a discount rate for low-income people. Any Planned Parenthood branch will also offer STI tests. Look up Planned Parenthood, and see if there are any branches in your area.

CHAPTER SIX
TALKING ABOUT FEELINGS

Let's talk about the open secret of dating: No one knows what they're doing. Everyone feels awkward. Even experienced adults are making up their approach to relationships as they go. There is no one-size-fits-all map to dating. Everyone has to draw their own map based on their own history, values, and desires.

The only tried-and-true remedy to combat awkwardness in dating is communication. You've gotta talk it out.

BRAVE PEOPLE OPEN UP

The name of the feelings game is honesty. It's hard to talk honestly about the things that affect us. People put off talking about big things (like coming out) and small things (like telling your boyfriend you don't like his favorite shirt). They're not sure what to say or how to say it. Some people spend a lifetime trying to find the right words to discuss their sexuality. Some people spend years in relationships they don't enjoy because speaking up about the problems seems terrifyingly impossible. Some people miss the chance (over and over and over) to build healthy relationships because they're too worried about rejection to take the leap of sharing their feelings.

Talking about feelings is the bravest and kindest way to be. You can't change how someone else feels. But you can express what's going on in your head. An excellent model for communications in relationships is an I-message. An I-message looks like this:

- "I feel . . . (name the feeling) when . . . (describe the behavior) because (explain the effect the behavior has)."
- "I feel disrespected when you don't use the pronouns I asked you to use because it makes me feel uncomfortable in my own body."
- "I feel upset when you interrupt me because it makes me feel as if no one cares about what I'm saying."

With "I" messages, the speaker shares their feelings without coming across as judging the other person. It shows that you want to exchange the facts, find a solution together, and seek a helpful or positive change in the situation. Being able to talk about things that are upsetting is a crucial skill in any relationship, whether it's with a partner, a friend, a parent, a coworker, or even a stranger. Angry, upsetting feelings that we ignore fester over time into resentment and even violence. That's a relationship killer. And a dangerous way to live in the world.

When asking someone to change a certain behavior, it helps to be really specific about what you want that person to do. Instead of telling them not to do something, suggest an alternative that would work better or make you feel better. For example,

- "I feel disrespected when you don't use the pronouns I asked you to use because it makes me feel uncomfortable in my own body."
- **Action:** I need you to use they/them pronouns when talking about me, even when I'm not in the room. Otherwise, you are misgendering me.
- "I feel upset when I'm interrupted because it makes me feel as if no one cares about what I'm saying."

- **Action:** When I'm talking, please wait for a moment and make sure I'm done before you begin.

On the flip side, if someone brings up a problem with your behavior, the most effective reaction is to listen. Acknowledge the other person's feelings, and even if it hurts to hear them, tell the person that you're glad they made the effort and took the risk to raise the issue. Responding well to criticism is super difficult. Try to hear what they're saying and think about what impact your behavior had on them. Slow down, take a deep breath before responding, and then try to talk about solutions.

For example,

- "I understand why my using the wrong pronouns to describe you would make you feel uncomfortable. Thanks for letting me know I was hurting you in this way. I screwed up your pronouns because it's difficult for me to remember to use the right words all the time, but I'll work harder to be more careful and considerate."
- "Thanks for flagging that I have a bad habit of interrupting you. I think I talk over you because I'm excited about what you're saying and want to add onto it. I definitely appreciate your ideas and opinions. I'll do better to let you finish your thoughts before I jump in."

KNOW TO SAY NO

Most of us, especially girls and women, are taught to be people pleasers and to put other people's needs first and our needs second. "Be nice!" is usually a message that we should do what other people want without complaint. But when you're trained to always say yes, it's hard to learn how to say no. It's hard to express what *you* want and to create healthy boundaries.

It's not only okay to say no, it's essential to say no! In intimate relationships, you have no obligation to agree to do anything with

TIPS FOR HARD CONVERSATIONS

Disagreement is a natural part of life. In any relationship—whether it's a friendship, a romance, at work, or with family members—conflict will occur. The real skill is to talk about the conflicts rather than ignoring them.

- **Ask yourself what makes you upset.** Get to the root of what's hurtful. Then you can pinpoint what's wrong and come up with possible solutions.

- **Focus on the problem, not the person.** It's easy to spiral from "you were late to pick me up" to "you're a terrible person!" Keep focused on the actual behavior that is irritating you without casting blame on the person as a whole, calling them names, or mocking them.

- **Work toward making a change.** Ask yourself, "What can this person do in the future to ease this problem? What can I do?" Try to agree on action steps. Change doesn't happen all at once. It often takes a long time to transform behavior. Patience is a big part of the communication game.

someone because you're worried about hurting their feelings if you say no. That includes going to a dance, making out, and having sex. It's your job to take care of your own body and feelings first. This means listening to your inner voice and listening to what your instincts and values tell you. If your instincts tell you that you don't want to do something or that it's unsafe to do so, you don't have to. It's not okay to make someone else happy by making yourself unhappy or unsafe.

Some of the boundaries you set are physical: deciding who is allowed to touch you and how, where you want to be touched and where you don't, what to put in your body (such as alcohol), how your body looks (such as whether to shave your legs or paint your nails), and what happens to your body (such as whether to start hormone therapy).

Other boundaries are emotional: deciding with whom you feel comfortable being vulnerable, with whom to share your identity and sexual history, with whom to say "I love you" or not, and when you can support someone emotionally and when you're maxed out.

Other boundaries are social: deciding with whom you'll spend time and how much, what you're interested in (such as whether to go to church, join the honor society, or study art), and what types of clothes to wear.

In dating, always respect your boundaries. If you want to do something, give enthusiastic consent. If you don't, say a firm no. The same is true in respecting other people's boundaries. Listen for enthusiastic consent. If someone seems uncertain, uncomfortable, or pressured in any way into going along with your desires, they're not enthusiastically consenting. If someone says "Umm . . ." or stays silent when you suggest something, that's not enthusiastic consent—that's a no. Take time, go slowly, and make space for anyone you're dating or interested in to express their feelings. If they say no to something you want to do, respect where they're coming from and don't push them to change their mind. People's boundaries change with time. But let them—not you—be the one to decide what changes and when.

HOW TO SAY NO

Having boundaries doesn't make you stubborn, mean, or selfish. Saying no is an articulate and valid way of expressing what you want. Establishing boundaries doesn't always mean actually saying the word *no.* Here are some options for saying no:

"My friend is having a birthday party. Want to come?"

"Thanks for the invite! I don't feel like going out. I'm feeling low energy, and I don't feel like meeting a whole bunch of new people."

"Will you go to prom with me?"

"That's really nice of you to ask. That makes me feel good. But I don't want to go with you. It feels too date-y, and I'm not into that."

"Do you want a beer?"

"Oh, no thanks, I'm going to stick to water tonight."

"Why are you spending your time with your friends instead of me? I'm your girlfriend, and you should always want to hang out just with me!"

"I really love spending time with you. It's important for me to have my own time too. My friends are a big part of who I am, and I want to spend time with them too."

"Do you see us ever becoming more than friends?"

"I think you're great. But I'm not attracted to you, so I don't want to date you."

"Honey, you would look so much prettier in a dress."

"Mom, I feel that I look good this way. Wearing pants makes me feel more comfortable and confident. This is what I'm going to wear."

"You don't want to have sex with me because you don't love me."

"That's not true. I love you, but I feel differently about sex than you do. I'm not ready to have sex. I want to move more slowly."

FEEL THE FEELINGS

Talking about positive feelings can be tough too. Sometimes it feels as if it would be easier to walk off a cliff than confess to a crush. Dating requires being brave, honest, and direct. That's not only because you'll get the feeling off your chest but also because discussing intimate things is necessary for respecting consent.

It's normal to have crushes on more than one person at a time. It's also normal to have a crush on only one person—or on no one at all. Attraction varies. Some people are attracted to lots of other people. Some are attracted to very few.

So, if you like someone, what do you do?

The best way to start is to ask them questions about themselves and their interests. Listen to what they say. If you're interested in some of the same things they are, get involved in the same groups at school so you can get to know each other better while also working on something you both care about. Make it clear how much they mean to you by supporting them. If they invite you to their play, soccer game, or charity fund-raiser, show up and cheer them on. Tell them they did a great job.

If there's a moment that feels appropriate, take the plunge and tell them (in words!) how you feel. This can be terrifying and awkward. But remember: Everyone is terrified and awkward.

Here are some ways to tell someone you like them, along with kind responses you can share if someone tells you they like you but you don't feel the same way about them:

"I know you like *Star Wars*. Do you want to go see the new movie with me?"

You might say,

- "Sure, I'd love to. Is it just you and me or should we bring friends?"
- "That sounds great, but I have to ask, is it a date? I like you, but I don't really feel like dating anyone right now."
- "That's really nice, thanks for thinking of me. But I actually already made plans to see it and I don't want to ditch them."

TERRIBLE FLIRTING ADVICE

A lot of bad flirting advice comes from pickup artists—guys online who make money by telling men how to flirt with women. Much of their advice is actually pretty malicious. They teach men how to engage in manipulation, deception, and hurtful behavior. They view women as prizes to be won rather than real humans who have their own desires and can make their own decisions. One common piece of pickup-artist advice is to engage in negging: insulting a woman so that her self-esteem is lowered and she feels more vulnerable. Another pickup-artist tactic is to touch women lightly on their shoulders or legs and see how they respond. These tricks might work to get someone to pay attention to you in the short term, but very quickly, they'll think you're a jerk.

"Hey, I know this is awkward, but I wanted to tell you that I really like you."

You might say,

- "Wow, that's awesome. I like you too."
- "You do? That's really nice. I don't know whether I'm attracted to you or not. I'm still figuring out my feelings."
- "Thanks for being honest. I like you as a friend, but I'm not attracted to you."

"It's been a really good night. Can I kiss you?"

You might say,

- "I'd like that."
- "Not tonight, that's moving too fast for me. Maybe I can take you up on that later?"
- "That's sweet, but I don't want to. I just don't feel as if it's a good idea for me."

WHEN SHOULD YOU *NOT* TALK TO SOMEONE?

Vulnerability is a strength. The more you can open up to trusted people around you, the deeper and more real your relationships will be. But you also get to decide what *not* to tell people.

Would you tell the cashier at the grocery store that you just had sex? How about your best friend? How about your mom? We all draw our own communication boundaries. When deciding what to share and with whom, think about these things:

- **Safety.** Would this person react in a way that could physically harm you?
- **Respect.** Do they respect you enough to listen to what you're saying and to believe you?
- **Relationship.** Are they the right person in your life to discuss this with? Some conversations you may only want to have with a parent, therapist, or medical

professional. Other conversations you may want to have with a long-term partner or best friend.

- **Support.** In what ways will the person be able to support you? What support can you seek out if they can't or won't help you or if they don't agree with your choices?
- **Communication.** When, where, and how is the best way to talk about this issue?

If you feel your safety might be in jeopardy, you don't have to have a conversation at all. For example, if you're worried a partner will become violent when you try to break up with them, that's a conversation you should not have face-to-face. Go to a place that feels safe, surround yourself with people you trust, and text or email what you need to say to your partner. Don't go it alone. Tell friends and family who can support you that you're breaking things off with your partner and you're worried they'll be violent. It's easier to stay safe if you have a support network around you.

Another example is if a parent might kick you out of the house or cut off funding for college if you come out to them. Then you're under no obligation to come out. You can wait however long it takes—weeks, months, or years—for you to be in a safe, stable, independent situation. Then start that conversation if it feels right and safe to you.

Many people feel a lot of pressure to be honest about absolutely everything. They worry that if they aren't honest, they are lying about their lives. But waiting to feel safe, respected, and supported by someone before you share something difficult is not the same as lying. You are building trust with another person, and that can take a long time.

Think hard before you speak up about an attraction you might feel for a coworker or roommate. You have to spend a lot of time with this person. If they tell you they don't share your feelings, your workplace or apartment can suddenly become a tough place to be. And if you supervise the person you're attracted to, definitely keep your feelings to yourself. The power dynamic is not equal, and approaching that person with your attraction is a form of sexual harassment.

Avoid speaking to someone who has asked you to stay away. This happens a lot after a breakup. One person will ask to not be in contact for a while. This request needs to be respected, even if it's tempting to pour your heart and soul into a text message at two in the morning. Ignore that urge. Instead of sending messages to someone who doesn't want to hear from you, write down your feelings in a journal, in a word document, or in draft emails, and then delete them.

When starting a tricky conversation, make sure you have the time and emotional energy to have the discussion. There's never a perfect time to bring up tough topics, but be aware of the stress the topic will cause. A classic bad move is bringing up a huge issue right before a big event. For example, on the thirty-minute drive with your boyfriend to his parents' house for Thanksgiving, you tell him you want to break up. Making a big decision during an emotionally turbulent time is another recipe for disaster. For example, deciding at three in the morning that you absolutely must text a longtime crush and confess your feelings. Better way to go? Slow down. Make sure that you have had enough food, water, and sleep to operate at full capacity and that you have enough time to talk through your feelings with the person.

ADDICTED TO LIKES

An important aspect of communication is how much of your brain is focused on the person you're talking to and how much is thinking about checking Instagram.

When was the last time you went a whole day without looking at your phone? A 2018 study from the University of Buffalo in New York found that students would much rather be deprived of food for three hours than their smartphones. But being apart from your phone for a few hours is good for your brain—and for your relationships and self-confidence.

According to Apple, the average iPhone user checks their phone eighty times a day. That constant distraction takes away from face-to-face relationships. In her book *Reclaiming Conversation*, sociologist Sherry Turkle of the Massachusetts Institute of Technology says that 89 percent of Americans took out a phone during their last social interaction, and 82 percent said that it deteriorated the conversation they were in.

Phones also distract us even when we're not looking at them. Our brains notice a phone when it vibrates or pings, even if we don't pick it up to look at it. One study by Florida State University researchers found that after hearing a phone vibrate or ring with an incoming text, people start thinking about what it might be and planning a theoretical response. In another study, University of California San Diego students were asked to take a test while their phones were either in front of them on their desks, stowed in their bags, or stashed in a different room. The results were clear: Students whose phones were in view had more trouble concentrating and solving problems. As the phone's proximity increased, brainpower decreased.

This ties into dating and relationships because it shows how hard it is to be fully present with another person when a phone is in the mix. To enjoy time with someone, whether it's a partner or your parents, stash the phone somewhere so you won't be hungry to check it.

Scrolling through social media can be destructive to your self-image. Instagram, Facebook, and Snapchat are marketed as positive places for friends to share their lives. The reality is that all those photos of other people looking pretty and having fun can be a toxic mirror. Research shows that teens who spend more time looking at social media are more frequently dissatisfied with their bodies. The constant life comparisons that apps invite can be demoralizing when you're unhappy and everyone else seems to be #blessed. Do yourself a huge favor and take breaks from your phone during the day or week. Leave it at your house when you go out or at least keep it in your bag or a back pocket instead of in your hand.

Sending sexy messages or photos can be fun—one in seven teens say they've sent a sext. Sending sexy text or photos isn't necessarily a problem if it's done with consent. The problem comes when consent is violated. The "unwanted dick pic" is a real phenomenon. Among men under the age of thirty-four, 24 percent say they have sent a dick pic to someone without being asked. It's not okay to flash your penis at a stranger, whether you're on the street or on your phone. When people demand photos of you or share photos of themselves without your asking for them, that's manipulative and exploitative behavior. It's just as bad as demanding to see a part of your body in real life. It's disrespectful and crosses a personal boundary.

The other huge problem around sexting and consent is when people forward private photos from someone to other people. That happens all the time. One in four Americans has shared sexy photos they've received with friends. So remember that when you send someone a photo, it's impossible to know where it will wind up. Even if the recipient doesn't share it, their

THE INTERNET NEVER FORGETS

Once an image is online, it's hard to remove it. Any image you share digitally—over Instagram, Snapchat, Facebook, texting, or email—can wind up posted somewhere else online. People often use the threat of posting private photos as a way to exploit and humiliate others. A 2016 survey of three thousand Americans found that one in twenty-five people has either been threatened with or actually had an explicit image shared online. Young women and LGBTQ people are more likely to be threatened with having an explicit photo shared without their consent, usually by vengeful exes or jealous adult men in their lives. Play it safe. Keep your sexy photos to yourself.

phone could be stolen or hacked. Some revenge porn websites profit from vengeful exes who upload photos of their former partners.

If you decide to sext, play it safe. Sharing pornographic photos of yourself could constitute child porn if you're under eighteen. People have been prosecuted with a felony for sexting when they or their partner is under eighteen. To be safe, never send erotic photos of yourself. Stick to sexy words instead. If you do really, really want to send a photo of your body, don't include your face. And only send someone that sext if they've made it clear they actually want it. Finally, delete any sexy photos you take and make sure your partner deletes any they receive and then empty the trash.

QUESTIONS TO THINK ABOUT

I'm sixteen and I had sex once before at summer camp. Now I have a boyfriend, and he says that since I'm not a virgin anyway, I should be fine having sex with him. But it feels different with him. I don't know. Am I being too stubborn?

You're not being stubborn. You're listening to your gut. Having sex with one person doesn't guarantee you want to have sex with someone else—even if you like that new person a lot! Sex with each person is a new decision to approach on a case-by-case basis. Whatever someone's reasons for wanting to move slowly on sex, those reasons are valid. A supportive partner will listen to you, respect your feelings, and not guilt you into changing your mind. Because he's putting pressure on you, your boyfriend is not being supportive of your boundaries or respecting how you feel. He needs to level up his respect, or you can leave him behind.

I'm a sophomore guy, and I'm pretty sure I'm gay. I came out to my parents last year and they were totally supportive, but my mom asked me not to tell my grandma. My grandma is a conservative Christian, and she'll probably be upset. My mom thinks she might not help me pay for college if I tell her. But I feel as if I'm lying. Should I tell my grandma and how?

Whether you tell your grandma is up to you, not your mom. But it's worth listening to your mom and weighing the pros and cons. How important is it to you that your grandma knows about this part of you? How will a negative response affect you? You are not lying by not discussing your identity. Your first responsibility is always to make sure you're doing what's necessary to protect yourself. Will you be able to attend college without your grandma's support? If not, how would it impact you emotionally to wait until you're done with college to come out? A good strategy is testing the waters by bringing up LGBTQ issues. Tell your grandma about a TV show with a gay character. Point out a news article about a gay pride parade. How she responds can be a clue to how she'd respond to your own news. She might surprise you. Then again you might not be in a position to take that risk.

CHAPTER SEVEN
DO WHAT FEELS GOOD

Sex isn't just about body parts. It's about feelings, emotions, and ideas. A lot of sex doesn't happen between your legs. It happens in your head. Human bodies are designed to feel good all over. People are sensitive to varying degrees all over their bodies, not just in their genitalia. Just like every part of sexuality, what feels good is different for everyone. Stroking, kissing, licking, or carefully biting or slapping these areas can drive someone wild. And on a different person, that action might not feel stimulating or might even feel bad.

Figuring out what feels good to you requires exploring with an open mind and listening to your body. Sex requires honest and clear communication. And keep in mind that what you like might not be what you expect.

SEX IS LIKE PIZZA
Sex educator Al Vernacchio says that it's ludicrous to describe sex as a baseball game—one where you get to first base by making out and then

where you hit a home run by having intercourse. That style of thinking divides the people participating into opposing, competitive teams. If you don't "score," you lose. That way of thinking about sex isn't only boring. It's dangerous. There's pressure to push your partner forward, ever forward, as fast as possible toward one goal.

In place of the baseball metaphor, Vernacchio offers a new one: sex is like pizza. You wouldn't invite someone over to your house and force them to eat pizza. You would ask if they want some first. Do they want one slice? Or a whole pie? Maybe they don't want pizza at all. If they do, you'd talk through topping options and come to mutual decisions. Do you feel good about mushrooms? Great. Would you want some pineapple? No? Okay. That's fine. Not everyone likes pineapple.

Relationships work the same way. Great relationships come in all kinds of flavors.

Writing the menu for your own relationships requires finding good relationship role models. Where do you see sexual, romantic, or asexual relationships like what you want? Who has a good balance of independence, loving support, and the ability to talk through hard times? Who seems to be great at laughing and having fun together? Who is good at ordering pizza together? What kinds of pizza do *you* want?

GETTING YOURSELF OFF

The safest form of sex doesn't involve anyone else at all—it's just you. Masturbation, or stimulating your genitalia for pleasure, is natural and normal. Many people masturbate from a very young age, before they even have the words to describe it. Some people masturbate by rubbing the head of their penis or their clitoris with their hand or fingers. Other people rub their genitalia on a pillow or balled-up T-shirt or with the flowing water in the shower or tub. It can also feel good to use a sex toy, like a vibrator, for stimulation.

The brain is as much a part of masturbation as the body. When people masturbate, they think about erotic images or tell themselves a sexy story. These fantasies don't always reflect what you want to do in real life. Fantasies are a safe way for your brain to explore sexuality. They don't mean you're perverted or broken or wanting that behavior IRL.

Most teens get themselves off at least once a month. Many do so more than once a week or even several times a day. Masturbation has a lot of health benefits. It reduces stress, helps the body relax, and helps people fall asleep. And it's super safe since there's no chance of getting yourself pregnant or giving yourself an STI.

WHAT IS SEX, ANYWAY?

Ask ten people to define sex, and you'll probably get ten different answers. That's because you can have sex many different ways.

You can have sex with your hands. The clitoris is the vulva's pleasure center. Only 25 percent of women orgasm, or reach sexual climax, through vaginal penetration alone. Most vulvas need clitoral stimulation to reach orgasm. A hand job is gripping a penis with your hand and rubbing it up and down.

You can have sex with your tongue. Stimulating a clitoris with your tongue ("going down on" or "eating out") feels great to many people. So does a blow job—sucking on a penis. Both of these are oral sex. About 70 percent of Americans have had oral sex by the time they are eighteen. You can spread STIs through oral sex, so take precautions.

MASTURBATION MYTHS

Masturbation does not

- cause blindness or acne
- make you sterile
- make you a sex addict
- make you go insane
- mean you're unnatural or perverted
- mean you'll never be happy with a sexual partner

You can have sex with sex toys. A dildo is a penis-shaped toy for inserting into the vagina or anus. Vibrators come in all shapes and sizes. They are usually battery-powered and vibrate to stimulate the clitoris or prostate (through the anus). Having sex with toys is also very safe because it doesn't carry the risk of spreading STIs. Definitely clean them with soap and water after use.

You can have sex with a penis and anus. Inserting the penis into the anus is anal sex. People of all genders and sexual orientations have anal sex. You can get and give STIs through anal sex, so be sure to wear a condom if you have a penis.

You can have sex with a penis and vagina. Inserting a penis into the vaginal opening is vaginal intercourse. This can result in pregnancy. You can get and give STIs from vaginal intercourse, so be sure to have protected sex.

Every type of sex requires three things:

- **Consent.** Talk about what you want and what your partner wants. Get verbal affirmation that everyone feels good about what's going on along the way.
- **Knowledge about STIs and protection.** Talk about any STIs you or your partner may have. Let your partner know when you were last tested and what the risks might be. Ask them when they were last tested. Err on the side of extreme caution. Use condoms if you or your partner has a penis to protect yourself from STIs, especially with new partners.
- **Water-based lubrication.** Do not have anal sex without lube. Without lube, it's very likely to tear the lining of the rectum. Adding extra lube to all the other types of sex (except oral, where your saliva will do the trick) is also a good idea. Don't use household items such as canola oil or Crisco for lube. That's messy, and they can be full of bacteria. Instead, buy personal lubricant from a sex shop,

drugstore, or online. You'll find all types to choose from, including flavored lubes. It can be fun to choose a lube with your partner!

ORGASM MYSTERIES

When genitalia is stimulated in just the right way, for just the right amount of time, and with just the right pressure, the whole body responds. The genitalia gets wet. Penises emit pre-cum and vaginas emit clear fluid, both help lubricate the skin. The more someone is stimulated, the more their heart rate speeds up, their breath gets quicker, and their muscles tense. Finally, the tension releases in an intense moment of climax, or orgasm, and it feels great. Afterward, people feel both relaxed and giddy.

Having an orgasm is not the same thing as ejaculating, but men often ejaculate when they have an orgasm. Women can ejaculate, too, though it's less common. So-called female ejaculation, or squirting, emits a clear fluid from the vagina during orgasm. People often mistake this fluid for pee, but it's not.

The brain is your body's biggest sex organ. What's happening in your head mostly determines whether you have an orgasm. An infinite number of factors influence whether someone will have an orgasm. The big things are that they need to feel comfortable and be sexually aroused. It's hard to have an orgasm if you're feeling stressed out or anxious. It's hard to have an orgasm if you're feeling uncomfortable about your own body, awkward with your partner, or pressured. Typically, everything needs to feel right.

Many people, especially women, take a long time to feel comfortable enough to have an orgasm with a partner. Many people don't have an orgasm when they're with a new partner. They need to build up trust and comfort with the person. Even in an established sexual relationship, partners don't always achieve orgasm each time.

People lie all the time about orgasming. In a *Cosmo* survey,

PORN MAY BE SEXY ... BUT IT'S NOT SEX ED

Many teens watch porn to fill in the gaps of their sex education. In a 2015 survey of British high schoolers, 60 percent said they had viewed porn to find out more about sex. The numbers are very similar among teens in the United States.

Porn is fake. It's not realistic sex, it's not realistic bodies, and it's not realistic relationships. Even on amateur sites, the people creating porn are professionals who are intentionally making a fantasy show, not a realistic how-to guide. In most porn, men are often impossibly muscular and have penises as large as broomsticks. Women have flawless skin and balloon-sized breasts. In heterosexual porn, women eagerly do whatever a man wants and never say no. No one gets sleepy, stressed out, or anxious. No one talks about consent, birth control, unwanted pregnancy, abortion, or STIs. Gay porn is the same. It's fantasy. While watching porn, it's easy to develop very unrealistic ideas about what sex looks like.

Yet among teens who have seen pornography, many viewers mistakenly believe porn is realistic. In an Indiana University survey, five out of six boys and three out of four girls believed that women in online porn were actually experiencing pleasure during sex scenes. The people in porn are actors. They're paid for their time and to put on over-the-top performances. Porn actors and models go through hours of makeup and styling to get their bodies (including their genitalia) looking perfect. Every sex scene has a team behind the scenes writing scripts, arranging lights, and digitally enhancing the footage so that everyone on-screen looks and sounds like an ideal human.

What you feel about porn and whether you decide to consume it depends on your values. Looking at porn doesn't make you sick or an addict. But don't hold yourself or your partners to the impossible standards of fantasy. Expect and enjoy the messy, sweaty, awkward reality.

67 percent of women said they had faked an orgasm at least once, mostly to make their partner feel successful. Having an orgasm is not about success or failure. Sex can feel good and be intimate without an orgasm. Not having an orgasm does not mean that you don't love your partner or that you're not attracted to them. It just means your body and mind are not working in unison at that particular moment. If you're frustrated at not being able to have an orgasm, the best thing you can do is let go of orgasm as a goal. Stressing out about orgasm actually hinders your ability to have an orgasm. Instead, take a break. Ask for a massage instead. Tell stories and laugh. Take it easy and try to relax. You can try again or wait for another time. Sexual intimacy, even without an orgasm, make people feel good.

WHAT TO EXPECT YOUR FIRST TIME

When, how, and with whom you have sex is entirely up to you. It comes down to your values. Think about what's important to you, your relationships, and how you feel. Talk to an adult that you trust, a medical professional, or a spiritual leader whose opinion you trust about what might be right for you.

States have laws specifying the legal age to have sex, ranging from sixteen to eighteen. These laws are designed to stop older people from preying on young people and talking them into having sex. If you're a teen and an older person is asking you to have sex, they may be breaking the law.

Here is a short checklist to help think about whether you're prepared, ready, and even wanting to have sex. If you decide to wait, go for it. You're in charge.

→ **Do you truly want to have sex?** Is having sex in line with your values, or would you feel as if you were betraying any part of yourself? Does it sound fun and exciting? If you feel pressure from a person, a group of friends, or society to have sex, that's not a good reason to start having sex. It's okay to say no.

RETHINKING VIRGINITY

People often think of virginity as a line in the sand. You're on one side of the line. Then you have penetrative sex, and you're on the other side. Virginity is more like a timeline that you walk along through life. There's a first time for doing a lot of sexual acts, so you're a first-timer over and over. It might be the first time you have penetrative sex with someone you love. It might be the first time you give someone oral sex or receive a blow job. Every sex act requires making a decision about whether it's right for you and feels good.

People talk about losing their virginity or taking someone else's. Sex should never be about losing and taking. That's an unhealthy power struggle. Having sex should be a mutual decision. You don't take someone's virginity or lose your own. You have consensual sex together.

$\longrightarrow$ **Do you know about the risks of STIs?** Talk to your partner about their history, and buy condoms if appropriate. If you're too embarrassed to get condoms, that's a sign you're not ready to have sex.

$\longrightarrow$ **Have you talked about pregnancy?** What will you do if you get pregnant? What will the other person do? Talk about birth control options, and if you need to, make an appointment with a doctor to talk about birth control.

$\longrightarrow$ **What are your feelings about abortion?** Talk to a trusted adult or doctor and to your partner about what would happen if you did get pregnant and if abortion would be part of the picture.

$\longrightarrow$ **Do you feel comfortable being naked?** Many people are self-conscious about their bodies. If you haven't been naked with your partner or you feel awkward about it, start by hanging out with them with few or no clothes on. Build trust by looking at your body and exploring your partner's, without the expectation of sex.

→ **Are you hoping sex will change your relationship?** Sometimes people jump into having sex because they think it will help them keep a partner or make their partner love them more. This never works. Only have sex if you want to, not to try to change a partner.

→ **Do you have a support network?** It's essential to have friends or family or professionals—or some mix of all of these people—to talk to about relationships and sex. They can help you figure out what's right for you and walk you through the mix of feelings that come up in any intimate relationship.

GOOD SEX REQUIRES LOTS OF . . . TALKING

The most important sign of whether you're ready to have sex is whether you and your partner can talk about sex. Whether you've been dating for years or just a few days, before you get physical, talk through your feelings. What are you excited about? What do you want to try? What are you worried about? What do you definitely not want to do? Talk about STIs and pregnancy risks.

Sex is often better the more you know each other's bodies. So try to hang out without having sex and explore each other's bodies. Basically any part of the body can be stimulated if you touch it in the right way. Massage can be a nice way to get to know each other's bodies. Play around and see what feels good.

The first time you have sex of any kind, keep your expectations low and your mind open. Penetrative sex often feels a little uncomfortable the first time, but it shouldn't hurt terribly. If anything is hurting, tell your partner to stop. Take a break, relax, talk, grab some more lube, and try again if you feel like it.

It is totally okay to change your mind in the middle of sex and decide you don't want to go any further. Your partner should respect that and not pressure you to continue. If your partner asks to stop, then stop. Listening to each other is an essential part of consent. Make space for your partner to speak up, and check in with them during sex. Ways to check in to ensure consent include asking, "How does this feel?" "Do you like this?" "What would you like to do?" "What's next?" Pay attention to your partner's nonverbal cues too. If they seem quiet, uncomfortable, or upset, stop having sex and take a break for a while.

Basically: Go slow. Check in. Talk a lot.

HOW CAN SOMEONE GET PREGNANT?

Pregnancy happens when a sperm fertilizes an egg. This can happen in a high-tech lab through artificial insemination, or it can happen through sexual intercourse. During intercourse, if semen gets into the vagina, the sperm cells can swim up through the cervix, into the uterus, and then into the fallopian tubes. Sperm live for up to six days. If they do connect with an egg during that time, healthy sperm will fertilize it. (When sperm fertilize two eggs, that's twins!)

Someone with a uterus can get pregnant any time sperm goes inside their vagina. That means you can't get pregnant from oral sex, anal sex, blow jobs, or hand jobs. But you *can* get pregnant any time you have penis-and-vagina sex. Here are some common myths about getting pregnant:

MYTH: *You can't get pregnant the first time you have sex.*

REALITY: Yep, you can. If you're having vaginal intercourse with a penis, it's possible to get pregnant.

MYTH: *You can't get pregnant if a partner pulls the penis out of the vagina (withdraws) before ejaculation.*

REALITY: Some ejaculate (pre-cum) seeps out of the penis even before ejaculation—and it does have sperm in it. A partner may promise to withdraw but then be overwhelmed with desire and ejaculate before they actually pull out. Out of every one hundred women who rely only on withdrawal, at least twenty-two to twenty-seven of them will get pregnant within one year.

MYTH: *You can't get pregnant if you use a condom.*

REALITY: If you use condoms perfectly every time you have sex, they're 98 percent effective at preventing pregnancy. But people are often a little sloppy in putting on and taking off condoms. In real life, condoms are about 85 percent effective. So about fifteen out of one hundred women who rely on condoms as their only birth control method will get pregnant each year.

MYTH: *You can't get pregnant if you have sex during your period.*

REALITY: Sperm can survive for six days inside the vagina. So they could still be there when an egg is released and you start your period.

MYTH: *Washing out your vagina through douching after sex will prevent you from getting pregnant.*

REALITY: Nope, that doesn't work either. Ejaculate has millions of sperm, and they swim so quickly up the vagina that no amount of washing can get them all out. And douching can increase your risk of infections, so don't do it.

It usually takes a few weeks for someone to realize they're pregnant. The signs of pregnancy are often mistaken for stress or sickness. Common symptoms of pregnancy are missing your period, having tender breasts, losing your appetite, feeling tired and nauseous, not being able to poop easily, and peeing more than usual. If you think you might be pregnant, people of any age can purchase a pregnancy test in any drugstore without a prescription and without ID. The kits provide results in a matter of minutes, and they are very reliable.

If you're pregnant, tell your parents or a trusted adult. Make an appointment to see a doctor. You can talk to your doctor about your options. You can see the pregnancy to term and raise the baby with your family, your partner, or by yourself. You can see the pregnancy to term and put the baby up for adoption. Or you can end the pregnancy with an abortion. Among unplanned pregnancies, 43 percent of people decide to end the pregnancy by abortion.

KNOW YOUR BIRTH CONTROL METHODS!

In the United States, half of all pregnancies are unplanned. Millions of teens and adult women every year get pregnant without meaning to. Among teens, the rates are highest: 74 percent to 95 percent of teen pregnancies are unplanned. If you don't want to get pregnant, use birth control! Don't rely only on withdrawal or the rhythm method (having sex on your least fertile days).

If you are going to have vaginal intercourse, make sure you and your partner prepare. Decide on a method of birth control. If you don't have one, figure out who will acquire it. Maybe you go to a pharmacy with your partner or by yourself to buy condoms. Maybe your partner buys them. Or maybe one of you makes an appointment at a clinic to start a regular birth control regimen.

Finding the right birth control method can take time and some trial-and-error. If you don't like one method, don't worry. You have at least twenty birth-control methods to choose from. All of them have pros and cons. Here's a rundown of the three most popular, nonpermanent contraceptive options in the United States. You can see a comprehensive list of the other options and their pros and cons at Bedsider.org.

Hormonal contraception methods aren't just for birth control. A lot of people use the Pill and IUDs to ease rough period symptoms, to even out their menstrual cycle, or to stop their periods altogether.

CONDOMS

Condoms are small pieces of latex that are rolled over the penis before sex. They're relatively cheap (about one dollar each) and prevent both pregnancy and the spread of STIs. When putting on a condom, be sure to roll it all the way down to the base of the penis. Otherwise, it might slip off. You and your partner can do this together if it feels right. After sex, hold onto the base of the penis so that the condom doesn't slip off when the penis becomes flaccid, or soft, again.

Condoms are the most common form of contraception. Some

people also use a second method of birth control because condoms do occasionally fail. Don't use two condoms at the same time. They will rub against each other during penetration and create a hole in the latex. Anyone, regardless of age, can purchase condoms at convenience stores, gas stations, pharmacies, and online.

THE PILL

Depending on which brand you buy, the Pill is a tiny dose of the hormone estrogen or of the two hormones estrogen and progesterone. Both change the menstrual cycle by stopping ovulation. The Pill does have downsides. One is that you have to take it every day for it to be effective—and it's easy to forget. Many people have side effects that come and go. Women on the Pill report it suppresses sexual desire, makes them moody or depressed, causes headaches, and spotting during periods. Not everyone experiences these side effects, however. You need a prescription to get the Pill, so make an appointment with a doctor or health clinic.

INTRAUTERINE DEVICES (IUDS)

If you want birth control that will last for years without having to think about it, the IUD could be a good choice. There are two kinds of IUDs: copper or plastic embedded with hormones. Hormonal IUDs release a low dose of progestin into the uterus, stopping ovulation. Copper IUDs create a small inflammatory reaction that is toxic to sperm and eggs, preventing pregnancy. A doctor at a clinic inserts the IUD through the vagina into the uterus. This is quick but often painful. Side effects—usually cramping and spotting—can last for weeks. The copper IUD can make periods longer and heavier. The hormonal IUDs can make periods shorter, lighter, or stop altogether. Copper IUDs provide contraception for twelve years. Hormonal IUDs prevent pregnancy for three to six years.

Accidents happen. Emergency contraception, usually sold under the brand name Plan B One-Step, is a pill to prevent pregnancy within three days of having sex. It's not as effective as other methods of contraception, but people often use it as their backup method if their first method of birth control fails, such as the condom breaks. Anyone can buy Plan B One-Step without a prescription at a drugstore.

Other common birth control options include
- a hormonal shot (brand name Depo-Provera),
- a hormone-laced plastic ring that's inserted into the vagina (brand name NuvaRing),
- a hormonal implant that's surgically inserted in the upper arm (brand name Implanon or Nexplanon).

Permanent forms of birth control include the tubal ligation for anatomical females. In this surgery, a doctor ties off the fallopian tubes through which eggs travel from the ovaries to the uterus. Anatomical males can choose a vasectomy. In this quick surgery, a doctor cuts,

Considerations When Choosing a Method of Contraception

Method of contraception	Effectiveness	STI prevention	Cost	Requires a health-care provider	Reduces periods
IUD	Great!	Not at all	Decent	yes	Pretty good
Implant	Great!	Not at all	Decent	yes	Great!
Shot	Pretty good	Not at all	Decent	yes	Great!
Pill	Pretty good	Not at all	Decent	yes	Great!
Diaphragm	Decent	Not at all	Pretty good	yes	Not at all
Condom	Decent	Great!	Pretty good	no	Not at all
Spermicide	Decent	Not at all	Great!	no	Not at all
Withdrawal	Decent	Not at all	Great!	no	Not at all
Fertility awareness (a.k.a. rhythm method)	Decent	Not at all	Great!	no	Not at all
Sterilization	Great!	Not at all	Pretty good	yes	Not at all
Emergency contraception	Decent	Not at all	Pretty good	yes	Decent

Great!   Pretty good   Decent   Not at all   ✓ yes   ▬ no

ties, or otherwise blocks the vas deferens so sperm can't leave the testes. (Yep, you will still experience orgasm after this surgery and you will still ejaculate.) Both of these surgeries have high rates of success in preventing pregnancy.

ABORTION

People have been performing abortions to end pregnancy for at least four thousand years. A medical text from ancient Egypt mentions gummy vaginal contraceptive substances made from honey, sodium carbonate, and crocodile dung! In the twenty-first century, you can skip the crocodile dung. This safe, legal procedure is done in a clinic or at home with doctor-prescribed pills. Almost all states have laws that regulate abortions, including requiring waiting periods, parental consent for minors (girls under the age of eighteen), and mandated counseling. For an up-to-date list of abortion laws in your state, check www.guttmacher.org. To find a clinic that provides abortions in your area, check the map at www.prochoice.org or call the National Abortion Federation hotline at 1-800-772-9100.

Insurance coverage and the cost of abortion depends on where you are and what health-care plan you have. The National Network of Abortion Funds (https://abortionfunds.org) helps individuals cover the costs of getting an abortion if they can't afford one.

In the United States, doctors perform abortions in two ways: either a two-pill medication abortion or an in-clinic surgical abortion. A medication abortion is available up to week 10 of pregnancy. The patient first meets with a doctor, who prescribes the two pills—mifepristone and misoprostol. You take one pill at the office and the other at home after the doctor's visit. During an in-clinic abortion, the patient goes into an exam room and medical professionals insert a thin tube through the cervix into the uterus. A suction machine removes the pregnancy tissue. Both of these options cause cramping and bleeding. The physical symptoms usually end within a day.

If you decide abortion is the best option for you, remember that you don't have to go through it alone. Ask a partner, a trusted parent or family member, or your best friend to go with you the day of the abortion. Ask them to stay with you that night and even the next day as you recover physically. Most people handle abortions just fine. Some women and teens find it helps to talk about their feelings with a counselor. You can too.

WHAT IS IT LIKE TO GET AN ABORTION?

People get abortions for all kinds of reasons. Some of the big reasons are the inability to afford to raise a child, knowing that having a baby would seriously interfere with work or school, because a person doesn't want to have a child with their partner, or because the pregnancy is the result of rape.

One in four women in the United States will get an abortion by the age of forty-five. People of all religions decide to get abortions. According to a 2014 survey of abortion patients by the Guttmacher Institute, 54 percent of abortion patients identified as Protestant or Catholic, 8 percent reported another religious affiliation, and 38 percent reported no religious affiliation. And the majority of women who get an abortion are already mothers.

If you decide on an abortion, the clinic should treat you with respect. The doctors and nurses should keep you informed about the process as they go and encourage you to ask questions. If they don't, find a different clinic. And bring someone you love and trust with you for support. You don't have to do this alone.

Here are some real-life anonymous abortion stories adapted from the website MyAbortionMyLife.org. Many more stories are on this website and on 1in3campaign.org.

> I was 16 just turning 17 at the time I became pregnant. It never hit me that something like this could happen to me. I was completely scared and thrown off. I was young, I had aspirations to go to college. I wasn't able to have a

baby. I made an appointment with Planned Parenthood. I remember having to drive all the way to Virginia to avoid being on a waiting list in South Carolina. I still hear the vacuum. God the vacuum. It was over. I was okay. Two years go by and I thought I never would have kids. But now I'm pregnant, six weeks along. I took so much from that experience. I value this baby more than I thought I could. You're not alone out there. I look back at the 17-year-old me and I applaud how strong she was.

I was a month shy of 16. My mom was in prison, my dad and I were barely on speaking terms. My boyfriend was that one person I could seek comfort from and confide in. We had dated off and on for three years, and we had sex for the first time. After weighing many options, I decided to get an abortion. I was facing zero assistance to cover my medical expenses and the electricity at the house was cut off. I was only 16, living alone with no money. I considered taking matters into my own hands to end my pregnancy, like throwing myself down the basement stairs. Thankfully, with the help of my father and grandparents, we scraped enough money together to go to the Planned Parenthood health center. After my abortion, my father drove me home.

CROSSING THE LINE: SEXUAL ASSAULT

No matter what you decide you do and don't want from your sexual life, remember this: It is never okay to have sex with someone who cannot give a conscious, reasoned, and verbal go ahead. It's never okay to have sex with someone who is drunk, asleep, or unconscious. Even if the person who wants to have sex with you is your boyfriend or girlfriend, they need to get your consent to sex every single time. And vice versa. Sex without consent is sexual assault. And it happens within relationships, when one partner manipulates or forces the other person into having sex and pressures them into saying yes even when they don't want to.

Sexual assault is common. According to the Centers for Disease Control and Prevention, about 7 percent of high schoolers say they have been physically forced to have intercourse when they didn't want to. When you expand the question beyond intercourse, the percentage more than doubles. During a one-year period, research showed that 16 percent of youth in the United States aged fourteen to seventeen had been sexually victimized, mostly by people they knew.

Here are two sexual assault stories:

When Katelyn and John first met, their relationship was complicated. John liked Katelyn, but he didn't want to have sex because he felt as if he wasn't in love. She kept trying to convince him and said that if John didn't sleep with her, she would break up with him and tell everyone he was a terrible boyfriend. John finally gave in and had sex with Katelyn. Although he had said yes, he realized later that he had been coerced.

David and Jenny watch a movie in their dorm room with some friends. They are attracted to each other. After the movie, everyone leaves and they're alone. Jenny flirts with David. She is excited when they start to make out. But then David pulls off her shirt and says he wants to have sex. Jenny, who has never had sex, is shocked and isn't sure what to do, so she just says nothing. David takes Jenny over to the bed, takes off her clothes, and begins to have sex with her. Jenny feels trapped. She wants to tell David to stop, but she doesn't want to make him mad. She lays still and is unresponsive during sex.

Both of these examples are sexual assault. In both, the person who wanted to have sex should have listened to their partner's verbal and nonverbal cues and respected their boundaries.

QUESTIONS TO THINK ABOUT

This is probably too personal and crazy, but when I get myself off, I often have really weird thoughts. Sometimes I imagine myself getting kidnapped by a celebrity and then he ties me up and makes me have sex with him. I would never want that to happen to anyone in real life. I'm anti-rape. So, why does my brain go there?

We can't always control what turns us on. Often what's not allowed by society is titillating precisely *because* it's wrong. Having those kinds of fantasies is normal. Thinking these thoughts doesn't make you someone who endorses rape. And it doesn't mean you want to do these things in real life. You could experiment someday safely with some of your fantasies, but don't feel as if your subconscious is telling you to act them out.

I'm sort of dating this guy. We just had a big talk about not becoming boyfriend-girlfriend. I think it would be nice to be his girlfriend, but he says it's important to him to be in an open relationship. I had no idea what that meant, so I just said okay. What is that?

An open relationship is an approach to dating that centers on non-monogamy rather than monogamy. In monogamy, someone has a romantic and sexual relationship only with one other person at a time. In non-monogamy, someone has romantic and sexual relationships with more than one person at a time. Both relationship structures come with their own advantages and disadvantages and require talking through boundaries and expectations. People who are in open relationships sometimes identify as polyamorous—*poly* means "many" and *amor* means "love." Open relationships are the right choice for some people, but if you're craving monogamy, it might not be the right choice for you.

CHAPTER EIGHT
YOU DESERVE TO BE HAPPY

Dating has always been evolving. In her book *Labor of Love,* historian Moira Weigel points out that what many people think of as a classic scenario—having a steady boyfriend or girlfriend—was shocking in the 1940s and 1950s. Parents, advice columnists, and even priests advised against going steady. Instead, they argued, it was better for young people to date around.

Throughout American history, every new generation has changed dating behaviors. Age, class, race, and gender shape what we see as normal. That men should pay for dinner, movies, and everything else on a date, for example, didn't come out of the blue. It became a norm because, for much of the twentieth century, women either weren't allowed to work outside the home or if they did, they were paid so little they could not afford to pick up the check. In 1900 women were paid half of what men were paid for the same jobs (and a wage gap continues).

These days, young Americans are continuing to change what relationships and dating look like. People are waiting longer to get married. The percentage of women who have decided not to have biological children has doubled since 1970, from one in ten to one in five. And younger people are more likely to define their sexuality as something other than straight. In a 2015 British survey, 43 percent of people aged eighteen to twenty-four identified themselves as not exclusively heterosexual. Only 7 percent of people over sixty identified that way. These trends show how people are making new choices about what healthy relationships look like to them.

All of this is to say that there is no right way to date. You get to shape your relationships in the ways that work for you and make you feel happy and healthy. That can mean following established rules or making up new rules—including deciding how to split the check.

YOUR BRAIN ON LUST

Beyoncé sings a song about the way love can make a person feel crazy. That's a reality a lot of people will recognize. Being intensely attracted to someone actually changes our brain chemistry. It feels exhilarating and all-consuming. That's in part because when someone is experiencing deep attraction, their brain releases higher-than-normal levels of the chemical dopamine and the hormone norepinephrine. These chemicals make people giddy, energetic, and euphoric. Neurological studies have found that attraction also seems to decrease serotonin, a chemical that's linked to regulating appetite and mood. Sexual arousal appears to turn off the critical-thinking regions in our brain that are tied to self-awareness and rational behavior.

When we're lusting after someone new, we're not our smartest selves. When making decisions about new relationships, know that your brain is essentially flooded with love drugs. It's not a good idea to make major, life-changing decisions (like moving across the country, getting married, getting pregnant, or getting a tattoo) within the first six months of falling in love with someone. Over time, brain chemistry evens out and that extra-loving dopamine and norepinephrine return to normal levels. That means your over-the-top feelings will shift with time too.

OBSESSION AND JEALOUSY ARE NOT CUTE

Keep an eye out for patterns of obsession. Someone who is obsessed with a crush or new partner will reorient their entire life around the person. They will drop things they're interested in to do stuff their crush likes instead. They might try to mold their personality to match what they think the object of their affection would be attracted to. They won't respect their own boundaries, values, or self-care. They risk losing themselves in pursuit of someone as a goal.

Obsession can also drive a dangerous behavior: stalking. The "no-just-means-try-harder" approach to relationships violates consent. Stalking involves trying to keep in constant contact, so it can take the form of following someone in person or digitally—like constantly texting and demanding to know where you are and who you're with. One in six women and one in nineteen men will be victimized by stalking in their lifetimes. If you feel that someone is stalking you, let someone you trust know, like a teacher or a parent. You'll need a support network to help keep that person away from you. Keeping yourself safe may require blocking the stalker on social media, asking sites to suspend their account, having their class schedule changed, or taking legal action.

Everyone gets jealous sometimes. Jealousy is a natural, universal human emotion, and it can be an important clue to our inner feelings. Keep an eye on the behaviors that make you or your partner jealous. Push yourselves to ask questions about the deeper root of those feelings. Usually at the core of jealousy is a feeling of insecurity. What are you or your partner insecure about? What are you afraid of? How can you reassure one another?

However, out-of-control jealousy can lead to controlling and abusive behavior. This type of jealousy includes accusing a partner of cheating or wanting to cheat, demanding frequent reassurance, and pouting or getting upset as a way to get attention. It also includes getting upset about spending any time apart, pursuing different interests, and monitoring a partner's communications.

If you find yourself acting in these ways, stop and check yourself. You can feel jealous without having to act on it. Use I-messages to bring up the issue with your partner and talk about what's causing the jealousy.

Jealous behavior often takes place over texts. Keeping in touch with your sweetie should feel thoughtful and positive. But constant contact can be a sign of possessive and jealous behavior. If they're using texts to keep tabs on where you are and who you're with, that's a red flag. Another problem sign is if your partner demands the right to go through your phone and read your texts—or opens your phone without your permission to see what you've been writing to other people or posting on social media. That's a violation of your right to privacy in a relationship. Good relationships are built on trust, and that means giving each other space and privacy.

LOVE IS RESPECT

If you are in a violent or emotionally abusive relationship, get help. You're not alone. And the abuse is not your fault. A lot of people stay in bad relationships because they're afraid people will judge them—either for leaving what looks from the outside like a "perfect" relationship or for staying so long in a bad situation. Once you've decided to end the relationship, stick to your resolve—abusive partners have a pattern of promising to change, apologizing for everything, being extra sweet and kind for a while and then slipping back into their hurtful ways.

Ending the relationship will be much easier with help and support. Ask a counselor, friends, and trusted adults to help you take steps to get your life back. If you want to talk to someone confidentially about abuse and your relationship, the go-to resource for teens is Love Is Respect. At www.loveisrespect.org, you can take quizzes to see if your relationship is abusive, live chat with a counselor, and find resources. You can call the teen hotline at 1-866-331-9474 or text "loveis" to 77054. All the Love Is Respect services are confidential.

If you are feeling monitored, overwhelmed, or threatened by someone's behavior or texts, that's a potentially toxic relationship. It's always okay to turn off your phone and ignore their texts. Try not to respond to harassing, abusive, or inappropriate texts. Instead, respond later that the messages were out of line. If you feel safe enough, you can bring up the problem in person and ask them to change their behavior. You can block phone numbers, and you can block people from being able to see your posts on social media. If they're threatening violence or making you feel unsafe, you and your family may decide to tell the police and seek a restraining order.

But, ultimately, those solutions require your action when really the problem is how the other person is behaving. It's ultimately their responsibility not to be abusive.

RECOGNIZING RED FLAGS

Everyone has the right to be happy and respected in a relationship. At a basic level, being in a relationship should feel good. But that doesn't mean being in love is always a happy feeling. People often think that all abusive relationships are violent. Sometimes, abuse is emotional, involving a pattern of behavior that one person uses against another to intimidate and to get what they want. That can mean making demands on their partner's time, shaming them, guilting them, or forcing them to do something they don't want to do, including sex.

So what does a healthy relationship look like? What does an unhealthy one look like? Here are lists of healthy, unhealthy, and abusive behaviors to think about. The lists adapt materials from the sexual health group Advocates for Youth and *The Teen Relationship Workbook.*

In a healthy relationship, people

- enjoy being with each other and are proud to be together
- add positively to each other's lives

- encourage each other's personal interests and individual goals, such as going to college, getting a job, or making art
- have some privacy, including being able to send texts or write in a journal without scrutiny
- accept responsibility for their actions and apologize when they're wrong
- feel as if they can be their whole selves, without hiding their identities
- treat their partner with respect and fairness
- can talk about their bodies and feelings about sex and gender
- treat each other as equals
- have shared interests
- have separate interests and identities
- disagree sometimes and talk through problems
- try hard to have honest and clear communication
- never hurt each other physically or sexually
- allow their partner space when needed

In an unhealthy relationship, people
- treat their partner disrespectfully and unfairly
- get extremely jealous or accuse the other person of cheating
- depend completely on the other to meet social or emotional needs

- withhold affection as a way to punish the other (such as giving them "the silent treatment")
- embarrass and humiliate each other
- frequently argue or fight, with partners yelling at each other and talking to their partner as if they're a child
- don't listen when the other person talks
- frequently criticize their partner's friends or family
- do things only with each other—they have no separate friends or interests
- try to control each other's clothing, actions, or interests, such as keeping someone from going to school or pursuing a dream
- blame the other partner for their own behavior (if you hadn't made me mad, I wouldn't have . . .)
- cheat on their partner
- use alcohol or drugs as an excuse for bad behavior

Signs of an abusive relationship are

- throwing or breaking things during an argument
- controlling what the other person does, such as making them feel bad for whom they see, what they wear, what they say, or what they're interested in

- threatening to hurt themselves or commit suicide if the other person breaks up with them
- being jealous often or overly jealous
- putting the other person down—calling them names or humiliating them
- exhibiting crazy-making behavior—one person lies or changes their story, or denies or minimizes the other person's experience. This behavior often makes the other person feel as if they are going crazy.

Do any of those behaviors sound familiar? If so, it's time to reevaluate your relationship.

People often blame the victim in abusive relationships, asking why they stayed or why they "let themselves" be treated in a bad way. That's unfair and actually makes the situation worse. People stay in unhealthy relationships for all sorts of reasons. They may be afraid of what their partner will do if they try to leave. If they don't have good role models for what a healthy relationship looks like, they may think that abuse is normal. They may be embarrassed about the abuse and feel as if they'll be judged if they tell people about it. They may love the person who is hurting them and hope that the abuser will change. They may rely on the abusive person for housing or financial support and feel as if they have nowhere to go if they leave.

Abuse happens in all types of relationships, including LGBTQ relationships. While women are more likely to be the victims of abuse, men and nonbinary people also can be victimized. Being in an abusive relationship does not mean there is anything wrong with you or that you failed in any way.

WHAT IF MY FRIEND IS IN A BAD RELATIONSHIP?

Supporting friends who are in unhealthy relationships is tough. They have to make the choice to stay or to go. You can be a good friend by helping them feel confident and loved. Make it clear that they deserve to be treated with respect.

- Listen to your friend, and ask how they're feeling. People in bad relationships often clam up and say everything is fine. Make space for honesty.

- Tell your friend that abuse is not their fault. Abuse hurts people's self-esteem, and many people feel stupid for being treated poorly. Make it clear that you are not judging them and are there to support them.

- Don't try to force a solution or confrontation. Follow your friend's lead. Don't push them into calling someone out or making the abuse public if they're not ready for it. This is their story to tell, not yours.

- Be careful what you post online. Your friend's abuser might be monitoring their social media and see your photos or posts. If you're unsure of what's okay to share, run it past your friend first.

BREAKING UP ISN'T A FAILURE

The hardest part of being in a relationship is knowing when it needs to end. Breaking up isn't a failure. It's actually really brave. Breaking up requires looking critically at your relationships and thinking through what's working and what's not. That's powerful. A breakup is not always an end. It's an evolution. Many people stay in each other's lives in a special and significant way even after they break up.

It can take a long time to decide whether to break up. Listen to yourself and trust your feelings. It helps to talk through your feelings with friends or family or a counselor. It also often helps to write out your thoughts.

Talk to your partner about the thoughts you're having. Bring up the problems you're noticing and how they're making you feel. You may be able to talk through them together and come to a positive solution. In long-term relationships, people talk through all kinds of problems over the years. The strength of a relationship isn't just in the good times. It's in the hard times too.

In the end, it comes down to one deceptively simple question: Do you want to stay in the relationship or not? If not, it's time to leave. No matter how tenderly you approach this, it will probably hurt. You'll probably both miss each other and feel sad, angry, and generally very upset. That's normal. But don't stay to avoid hurting the other person. It's not fair to them or to you.

Here are some tips for developing a breakup action plan:

- Get support by talking to your friends and family about how you're feeling. Let them know what's going on. Counselors can help too.
- Breaking up in person is the most respectful way to go about it, even though it's hard. If you're worried their reaction will be too dramatic, choose a public place to meet. That's often a way to make sure emotions don't get out of hand. If you don't feel safe meeting in person, you can send a breakup text or an email spelling out your decision.
- Tell your partner what you're unhappy about and why you need to leave. You don't have to justify every feeling. Don't feel bad if you can't always explain what you feel. But you do owe your partner some explanation. It's unkind and disrespectful not to.
- If you feel like sending your ex regretful or sentimental messages after the breakup, don't. Save those notes in a drafts folder or journal instead.

If the breakup isn't mutual and you're the one who feels dumped, here's a guide to dealing with the loss of a relationship you loved:

- Seek support from friends, family, or a counselor.
- Accept your partner's decision, and don't fight it. You

may think that the person breaking up with you is totally wrong or misguided, but it's their decision to make the life they want.

- Take space for yourself to process your sadness. Can you be friends with exes? Of course! You get to do whatever feels good to you. But many people immediately want to be friends after a breakup. Try taking some time apart first to see how you feel on your own.

- Find positive ways to grieve. Many people cope with sad feelings in destructive ways—with drugs and alcohol or by immediately starting up new relationships on the rebound. Find positive ways to deal with the sadness instead. Use that fuel of sadness to create art, power your athletics, or express compassion to others.

- Get enough sleep, eat three meals a day even if you don't feel like eating, and leave the house even if you don't feel like leaving the house. It's totally okay to wallow in sad songs and dark feelings, but go about the business of continuing your life while you're hurting.

- Keep a journal of your feelings. It's a great way to release grief and to process what you are going through.

- Breakups often hurt for a long time. It doesn't matter whether the relationship was one month or one year. There's no equation to determine how long you'll feel heartsick. Over time, the pain starts to be less ferocious and eventually fades so it's easier to live with.

The most important thing after a breakup is to take care of yourself! Build new routines that will be a scaffold for your changed life. Immerse yourself in an activity you love, take pleasure in your family and friends, foster new friendships, and keep yourself healthy. Use the breakup to reflect on your own relationship patterns. Think about what you did really well and what you could have done better in the relationship. Ask yourself what lessons you want to bring to the next one. Use what you've learned to continue to write the script for the relationships you want for yourself in your life. You are in charge!

QUESTIONS TO THINK ABOUT

My girlfriend and I broke up a year ago, and I still feel really sad about it. All my friends say I need to just get over her, but I miss her a lot sometimes. Is it normal to still feel sad a year after a breakup?

Does every sad song on the radio sound as if it's playing just for you? That's normal. There's no time limit on how long it takes to grieve a relationship. It sounds as if this was a significant relationship for you, so you'll probably be thinking about it for the rest of your life. But to move on, don't let it define your life. Seek out activities you're into and surround yourself with friends who get you. This relationship was one part of who you are. Foster the rest of you.

Last year, I was in a bad relationship with a boyfriend and I got pregnant. I decided to get an abortion, which was a really tough decision. Now, I'm in a new relationship with a great guy. Do I need to tell him about my abortion? And when?

You're under no obligation to tell anyone about your personal decisions if you don't want to. If you feel safe, comfortable, and supported in this relationship, there probably will be a time when you feel good about opening up about this history. But that decision needs to come from you. Not telling him doesn't mean you're lying. It means you're still processing what this experience means to you and how to talk about it.

ableism: discrimination or prejudice against people with disabilities. This can be pervasive in all parts of culture, from media (portraying disabled people as villains), to social interactions (making jokes about someone who is developmentally disabled), to policy (not requiring public schools to be accessible to people who use wheelchairs).

abortion: the deliberate ending of a pregnancy

asexuality: also called ace; a sexual orientation used to describe people who do not experience sexual attraction. Asexuality is a spectrum, so it describes a range of identities, from people who are sexually attracted only to a very small number of people over their lives to those who never experience sexual attraction.

birth control: the practice of preventing unwanted pregnancies, especially with contraception, such as condoms, pills, and implants containing hormones

birth control pill: also called the Pill; a daily hormonal pill that prevents pregnancy. The pill can be progestin or both progestin and estrogen. Birth control pills stop ovulation so that the female body does not release an egg.

bisexual: also called bi; people who experience enduring physical and sexual attractions to people of their same gender and other genders (regardless of whether they've ever acted on those attractions)

body positive: the belief that all human beings should be able to celebrate and appreciate their own bodies and the bodies of others, regardless of weight, height, size, and other physical features

cisgender: also called cis; someone who identities with the gender their family and doctors assigned them at birth based on an assessment of biological anatomy. *Cis* is a Latin prefix meaning "on the same side."

clitoris: this organ, which is both inside and outside the body, is the highly sensitive pleasure center of the vulva

come: a slang term for orgasm or ejaculation. It is often spelled cum.

consent: an agreement to do something or to give permission for something to happen. All sexual activity—kissing, touching, and intercourse—requires the enthusiastic consent of each person involved. Consent is a verbal exchange that happens when someone is sober, awake, conscious, and able to make a reasoned decision.

ejaculation: a quick discharge of genital fluid, like semen or vaginal fluid. It often, but not always, occurs with an orgasm.

gender expression: external or verbal cues to someone's gender that are shown by their clothes, makeup, hairstyle, name, pronouns, and the many other physical characteristics that shape how we present ourselves to and are perceived by others

gender fluid: also called genderqueer; a form of gender identity where someone does not identify with a single gender, moving naturally among genders

gender identity: a person's internal, deeply held sense of their gender, regardless of anatomical features

gender transition: moving from one gender to another. Depending on the person's individual identity and goals, gender transition can occur through changes to gender expression with no medical intervention at all, by taking the hormones estrogen or testosterone, through gender confirmation surgeries, or through some combination of various options. Hormonal and surgical procedures take place with the guidance of a doctor.

genitalia: human reproductive and sexual organs. Genitalia varies significantly in size, shape, and sensitivity.

harassment: being treated in an unwanted way because of your identity. Unwanted remarks about your body, clothes, or sexual activity, for example, are a form of sexual harassment.

heterosexism: discrimination in culture and the law based on the belief that heterosexuality is the only normal and acceptable sexual orientation

heterosexual: usually referred to as straight, heterosexual people feel physically and emotionally attracted to people of a gender other than their own. This includes a woman who is attracted exclusively to men or men who are exclusively attracted to women.

homophobia: dislike of or prejudice against people who do not identify as heterosexual

homosexual: a person who feels physically and emotionally attracted to people of their same gender

intersex: an umbrella term describing people born with reproductive and sexual anatomy, a chromosome pattern that doesn't seem to fit the clinical, medical definitions of male, female, or both

labia: part of the vulva, these flaps of sensitive skin have lots of nerve endings and surround the vaginal opening

LGBTQ: lesbian, gay, bisexual, transgender, queer or questioning. People sometimes add *A* (for asexual, allies, or both) and *I* (for intersex).

masturbation: the act of a person bringing themselves sexual pleasure

menstruation: also called a period, this is the shedding of the uterine lining that happens roughly every month. The liquid released during menstruation includes blood, mucus, and other fluids.

misgender: the act of referring to a person using a word, pronoun, or title that does not accurately describe their gender. For example, calling a woman "sir," or calling someone who uses they/them pronouns "he" or "she."

nonbinary: also called NB, or enby; technically meaning "not composed of just two things," this term describes the gender identity of people who fall outside the categories of male and female. Many nonbinary people use the pronouns they/them.

oral sex: use of the mouth or tongue for sexual stimulation. Common types of oral sex include cunnilingus (a mouth on the vulva), fellatio (a mouth on the penis), and anilingus (a mouth on the anus).

orgasm: an intense physical and mental experience of pleasure that is the result of physical stimulation or sexual fantasy. Orgasms typically involve muscle spasms and a delicious feeling of a release of tension.

ovulation: the day about once a month in the human fertility cycle where the ovary releases an egg. This day and roughly the five days beforehand are when someone is most likely to get pregnant if the egg contacts sperm.

polyamory: people who are attracted to multiple people at one time and have consensual relationships that involve multiple partners

pregnancy: when an egg cell (ovum) has been fertilized by sperm, the egg cell divides into multiple cells, and the fertilized egg implants in the lining of the uterus. If the process continues, the cells will continue to divide until they form an embryo.

premenstrual syndrome (PMS): mood swings, bloating, headaches, and other symptoms that some women experience before the onset of their period

puberty: the wide range of physical, emotional, and sexual changes that happen as humans' bodies change from childhood to adulthood. The changes are caused by fluctuating hormones, and the process lasts several years.

queer: a term people use to describe themselves when their sexual orientation is not exclusively heterosexual

racism: prejudice or discrimination directed against someone of a different race based on the belief that one's own race is superior. Racism includes both individual acts and society-wide systems that create inequality.

rape: when someone does a sexual act to someone else who does not freely consent to the act. Rape can happen to anyone of any age and gender.

sexism: prejudice, stereotyping, or discrimination, typically against women, on the basis of their sex

sexual assault: any type of sexual contact or behavior that occurs without the explicit consent of the recipient. This can include touching, groping, kissing, or any other unwanted activity.

sexually transmitted infection (STI): diseases that can be spread through sexual contact when one person's body fluids, like semen, come into contact with another person's mouth, vulva, or anus

sexual orientation: a person's sexual identity in relation to the gender they are attracted to. For example, a woman whose sexual orientation is lesbian is attracted to other women.

transgender: also called trans; someone whose gender does not match the gender their family and doctor assigned to them at birth

tubal ligation: a form of permanent birth control where the fallopian tubes are cut, blocked, or tied by a doctor to prevent fertilization

vasectomy: a form of permanent birth control in which a surgeon cuts the vas deferens tube in the penis to prevent sperm from being in semen

virginity: the state of never having experienced sexual activity. Virginity is different for each person, since everyone determines what they consider to be sex for themselves.

SOURCE NOTES

10   "What Is Consent?," University of Michigan Sexual Assault Prevention and Awareness Center, accessed June 29, 2016, https://sapac.umich.edu/article/49.

13   Emily Nagoski, *Come as You Are: The Surprising New Science That Will Transform Your Sex Life* (New York: Simon & Schuster, 2015), 32.

16   Heather Corinna, *S.E.X.: The All-You-Need-to-Know Sexuality Guide to Get You through Your Teens and Twenties* (New York: De Capo, 2016), 28.

21, 23 Malakai_the_peacock, "Transgender People of Reddit, What Was the First Memory or Sign That You Were Trans?," Reddit, accessed April 30, 2019, https://www.reddit .com/r/AskReddit/comments/6shoxk/serious_transgender_people_of_reddit_what _was_the/.

22   "Gender Nation Glossary." Refinery29, June 1, 2018, https://www.refinery29.com /lgbtq-definitions-gender-sexuality-terms.

24   Alfred Kinsey, *Sexual Behavior in the Human Male* (Bloomington: Indiana University Press, 1948), 639, https://www.kinseyinstitute.org/research/publications/kinsey -scale.php.

25   Juno Dawson, "This Book Is Gay," (Naperville, IL: Sourcebooks, 2015), 11.

26   Queen Mary, University of London, "Homosexual Behavior Largely Shaped by Genetics and Random Environmental Factors," ScienceDaily, June 30, 2008, https://www .sciencedaily.com/releases/2008/06/080628205430.htm.

28   Karin Miller, "Here's Why One Boob Is Sometimes Bigger Than the Other," *Self*, November 2, 2017, https://www.self.com/story/one-boob-bigger-than-the-other/.

30   "The 3 Scariest Words a Boy Can Hear," *NPR, All Things Considered*, July 14, 2014, https://www.npr.org/2014/07/14/330183987/the-3-scariest-words-a-boy-can-hear.

30   *The Mask You Live In*, directed by Jennifer Siebel Newsom (Los Angeles: Representation Project, 2015), 97 min. http://therepresentationproject.org/film/the-mask-you-live -in-film/.

33   D. Callander, C.E. Newman, and M. Arch Holt, "Is Sexual Racism Really Racism?," Sexual Behavior 44 (2015): 1991, https://doi.org/10.1007/s10508-015-0487-3.

34–35   Gemma Hartley, "Women Aren't Nags—We're Just Fed Up," *Harper's Bazaar*, September 27, 2017, https://www.harpersbazaar.com/culture/features/a12063822 /emotional-labor-gender-equality.

35   Dana Dovey, "Pretty Pretty Princess: Overexposure To Disney Culture May Affect Girls' Perceptions Of Body Image Throughout Life," *Medical Daily*, June 24, 2016, https://www.medicaldaily.com/pretty-pretty-princess-disney-princess-body-image -self-esteem-gender-390494.

35   Kelsey Miller, "Study: Most Girls Start Dieting by Age 8," Refinery 29, January 26, 2015, https://www.refinery29.com/2015/01/81288/children-dieting-body-image.

35   "Girls' Attitudes Survey 2016," Girlguiding, accessed July 2018, https://www.girlguiding
      .org.uk/globalassets/docs-and-resources/research-and-campaigns/girls-attitudes
      -survey-2016.pdf.

37   Stacy Smith et al, "Inequality in 900 Popular Films," USC Annenberg Media, Diversity,
      and Social Change Initiative, July 2017.

38   Emily Nagoski, *Come as You Are* (New York: Simon & Schuster, 2015), 159.

38   Nagoski, 161.

40–41 Pam O'Brien, "How Camila Mendes Stopped Fearing Carbs and Broke Her Dieting
      Addiction," Shape, October 11, 2018, https://www.shape.com/celebrities/interviews
      /camila-mendes-riverdale-overcame-fear-carbs-stopped-dieting.

59   James Myhre and Dennis Sifris, "Why HIV Rates Are High in African American
      Communities," VeryWell Health, accessed April 30, 2019, https://www.verywellhealth
      .com/why-hiv-rates-are-high-in-african-american-communities-4151837.

90–91 Anonymous, "I Was 16, Just Turning 17 at the Time," MyAbortionMyLife.org, July 1, 2018,
      https://www.myabortionmylife.org/single-post/2018/07/01/I-was-16-just-turning-17
      -at-the-time.

91   Anonymous, "Our Lives Are Created by the Choices We Make and Those That Are Made
      for Us," MyAbortionMyLife.org, February 28, 2017, https://www.myabortionmylife
      .org/single-post/2017/02/28/Our-lives-are-created-by-the-choices-we-make-and
      -those-that-are-made-for-us.

SELECTED BIBLIOGRAPHY

Bell, Ruth. *Changing Bodies, Changing Lives: A Book for Teens on Sex and Relationships*. 3rd ed. New York: Harmony, 1998.

Dusenbery, Maya. *Doing Harm: The Truth about How Bad Medicine and Lazy Science Leave Women Dismissed, Misdiagnosed, and Sick*. New York: HarperCollins, 2018.

Hasler, Nicole. *Sex: An Uncensored Introduction*. San Francisco: Zest Books, 2015.

Katz, Jackson. *The Macho Paradox: Why Some Men Hurt Women and How All Men Can Help*. Naperville, IL: Sourcebooks, 2006.

Keyser, Amber, ed. *The V-Word: True Stories about First-Time Sex*. Hillsboro, OR: Beyond Words, 2016.

Marcus, Eric. *Making Gay History: The Half-Century Fight for Lesbian and Gay Equal Rights*. 2nd ed. New York: Harper Perennial, 2002.

Myhre, James and Dennis Sifris. "Why HIV Rates Are High in African American Communities." VeryWell Health. Accessed January 2019. https://www.verywellhealth.com/why-hiv-rates -are-high-in-african-american-communities-4151837.

Owens-Reid, Danielle, and Kristin Russo. *This Is a Book for Parents of Gay Kids: A Question & Answer Guide to Everyday Life*. San Francisco: Chronicle Books, 2014.

Ryan, Christopher, and Cacilda Jetha. *Sex at Dawn: How We Mate, Why We Stray, and What It Means for Modern Relationships*. New York: Harper Perennial, 2011.

Stryker, Kitty, and Carol Queen. *Ask: Building Consent Culture*. Portland, OR: Thorntree, 2017.

Traister, Rebecca. *All the Single Ladies*. New York: Simon and Schuster, 2016.

Wolf, Naomi. *The Beauty Myth: How Images of Beauty Are Used against Women*. 2nd ed. New York: Harper Perennial, 2002.

FURTHER INFORMATION

TWENTY-PLUS GREAT REAL-LIFE STORIES TO READ

Arceneaux, Michael. *I Can't Date Jesus: Love, Sex, Family, Race, and Other Reasons I've Put My Faith in Beyoncé.* New York: Atria, 2018.

Baker, Jes. *Things No One Will Tell Fat Girls: A Handbook for Unapologetic Living.* New York: Seal, 2015.

Bechdel, Alison. *Fun Home: A Family Tragicomic.* Boston: Houghton Mifflin, 2007.

Blow, Charles M. *Fire Shut Up in My Bones: A Memoir.* Boston: Mariner Books, 2015.

Bornstein, Kate. *Gender Outlaw: On Men, Women and the Rest of Us.* Abingdon, UK: Routledge, 1994.

Brosh, Allie. *Hyperbole and a Half: Unfortunate Situations, Flawed Coping Mechanisms, Mayhem, and Other Things That Happened.* New York: Touchstone Books, 2013.

Chung, Nicole. *All You Can Ever Know: A Memoir.* New York: Catapult, 2018.

Conley, Garrard. *Boy Erased: A Memoir of Identity, Faith, and Family.* New York: Riverhead Books, 2017.

Cronn-Mills, Kristin. *Transgender Lives: Complex Stories, Complex Voices.* Minneapolis: Twenty-First Century Books, 2015.

Gay, Roxane. *Hunger.* New York: HarperCollins, 2017.

Irby, Samantha. *We Are Never Meeting in Real Life.* New York: Vintage, 2017.

Khakpour, Porochista. *Sick: A Memoir.* New York: Harper Perennial, 2018.

MariNaomi. *Kiss & Tell.* New York: Harper Perennial, 2011.

McBee, Thomas Page. *Man Alive: A True Story of Violence, Forgiveness and Becoming a Man.* San Francisco: City Lights Books, 2014.

Mock, Janet. *Redefining Realness: My Path to Womanhood, Identity, Love & So Much More.* New York: Atria Books, 2014.

Newlevant, Hazel. *Comics for Choice.* Cupertino, CA: Alternative Comics, 2017.

Noah, Trevor. *Born a Crime: Stories from a South African Childhood.* New York: Penguin Random House, 2016.

Rae, Issa. *The Misadventures of Awkward Black Girl.* New York: 37 Ink, 2016.

Robinson, Phoebe. *You Can't Touch My Hair: And Other Things I Still Have to Explain.* New York: Penguin Books, 2016.

Slater, Dashka. *The 57 Bus: A True Story of Two Teenagers and the Crime That Changed Their Lives.* New York: Farrar, Straus & Giroux, 2017.

Valenti, Jessica. *Sex Object: A Memoir.* New York: William Morrow, 2017.

West, Lindy. *Shrill: Notes from a Loud Woman.* London: Quercus, 2017.

TEN YOUTUBE CHANNELS TO WATCH

Feminist Frequency
https://www.youtube.com/user/feministfrequency
Created and hosted by Anita Sarkeesian, Feminist Frequency is an ongoing series that explores gender representations, myths, and messages in popular culture media—especially in video games.

Jake Edwards
https://www.youtube.com/user/JakeFTMagic
Edwards is a nonbinary, bisexual, panromantic human who sings songs and talks about their life.

Kati Morton
https://www.youtube.com/user/KatiMorton
This licensed therapist educates viewers about mental health disorders and answers tough questions about topics such as anxiety, eating disorders, and depression.

Kiera Rose
https://www.youtube.com/user/ScarletSaintOnline
Rose talks about houseplants, thrift store finds, and vegan recipes. She also delves into discussions of her bisexuality and mental health disorders, including several videos on the compulsive disorder dermatillomania.

MTV Decoded
https://www.youtube.com/user/mtvbraless
MTV Decoded is a weekly series where the fearless Franchesca Ramsey talks about race, pop culture, immigration, and gender. She is funny and thought-provoking.

Pidgeon
https://www.youtube.com/user/pidgejen
Pidgeon grew up believing they were the only intersex person in the world. They talk about their experience being diagnosed and undergoing operations as a child and then coming to terms with being intersex, queer, and nonbinary as an adult.

Princess Joules
https://www.youtube.com/user/princessjoules
Julie Vu, a.k.a. Princess Joules, is a Canadian transgender woman who gives fashion and makeup tutorials while also talking about transgender issues.

SkylarkEleven
https://www.youtube.com/user/skylarkeleven
In 2009, at the age of seventeen, Skylar started documenting his transition from female to male, showing his experiences injecting testosterone, getting gender confirmation surgery, and hearing his voice drop. He also makes music and shares his art.

Stevie Boebi
https://www.youtube.com/user/SassiBoB
On her YouTube channel, Stevie discusses body positivity, gives lesbian sex advice, and tells funny stories.

Vox's Strikethrough
https://www.youtube.com/user/voxdotcom
Hilarious host Carlos Maza analyzes media.

TEN INSTAGRAM ACCOUNTS TO FOLLOW

Amplifier Foundation
@amplifierart

Dedicated to changing the world through art, the Amplifier Foundation hires artists to make iconic political posters.

Bex Taylor-Klaus
@Bex_tk

The gay, nonbinary actor featured in films such as *Dumplin'* and *Discarnate* often struts down the red carpet in classy custom suits and poses for upbeat selfies.

Gemma Correll
@gemmacorrell

An illustrator who loves pugs and puns, Correll often also shares relatable drawings about mental health.

LGBT History
@LGBT_History

This account shares historic photos of LGBT activism and activists in the United States with lengthy captions that explain the backstory.

Mona Chalabi
@monachalabi

Visual journalist Mona Chalabi makes colorful graphs and charts that show things such as the average body hair and the history of interracial marriage.

Project Consent
@projectconsent

Through words and pictures, Project Consent supports sexual assault survivors to end violence.

Ruben Guadalupe Marquez
@broobs.psd

The queer artist immortalizes people who are his heroes in beautiful collages.

Them
@them

This magazine highlights LGBTQ fashionistas, artists, and creators from around the world.

The Vulva Gallery
@the.vulva.gallery

A collection of illustrations of bodies that showcases realistic and artistic drawings of vulvas.

You're Welcome Club
@yourwelcomeclub

This illustrator's body-positive account centers on celebrating diversity.

TEN PODCASTS TO LISTEN TO

Call Your Girlfriend

https://www.callyourgirlfriend.com

Long-distance best friends Aminatou Sow and Ann Friedman dish on this week in pop culture and highlight women who are agents, creators, movers, and shakers who have smart, interesting things to say.

Code Switch (*NPR*)

https://www.npr.org/sections/codeswitch

A team of journalists fascinated by the overlapping themes of race, ethnicity, and culture explore how they play out in Americans' lives and communities.

Gender Reveal

http://gender.libsyn.com/

Nonbinary host Molly Woodstock interviews LGBTQIA+ artists, activists, and educators; analyzes current events; and get a little bit closer to understanding what the heck gender is.

Latino USA (*NPR* and Futuro Media Group)

http://latinousa.org

Veteran journalist Maria Hinojosa shares stories about Latino people in the United States.

Making Gay History (Pineapple Street Media)

https://makinggayhistory.com

Host Eric Marcus shares tear-jerking oral histories recorded with LGBTQ pioneers in the 1980s.

Nancy (WNYC)

https://www.wnycstudios.org/shows/nancy

Two queer Asian American hosts share funny, sweet, and compelling stories about LGBTQ experiences in the United States.

Pod Save the People (Crooked Media)

https://crooked.com/podcast-series/pod-save-the-people

Host DeRay Mckesson is an activist and community organizer who has deep conversations about social, political, and cultural issues.

Popaganda (Bitch Media)

https://www.bitchmedia.org/feminist-podcasts

This feminism and pop culture podcast digs deep on issues of race, class, and gender in movies, books, music, films, and TV.

Queery (Earwolf)

https://www.earwolf.com/show/queery

Comedian Cameron Esposito chats with high-profile LGBTQ guests, including actors, drag queens, and movie producers.

Unladylike

https://unladylike.co/podcast/

From abortion rights to Lisa Frank, research-obsessed hosts Cristen Conger and Caroline Ervin delve into feminist issues.

TEN WEBSITES TO CHECK OUT

Besider

https://www.bedsider.org

Besider is an online birth control support network for women eighteen to twenty-nine that works to ensure that every young person has the power to decide if, when, and under what circumstances to get pregnant.

Bitch Media

https://www.bitchmedia.org

Over its twenty years as a magazine, *Bitch* has connected the dots between feminism and representation in pop culture.

Everyone Is Gay

http://everyoneisgay.com

This site offers friendly advice and insight on what it's like being an LGBTQ young person, including answering reader questions.

Go Ask Alice!

https://goaskalice.columbia.edu

Go Ask Alice! is a health question and answer internet resource featuring anonymous questions submitted by readers and curious minds.

It's Your Sex Life

http://www.itsyoursexlife.com

MTV's public information campaign about health and sexuality aims to reduce unintended pregnancies and prevent the spread of STIs.

Muslim Girl

http://muslimgirl.com

Muslim Girl publishes writings by young Muslim women on fashion, family, and politics.

Remezcla

http://remezcla.com

Remezcla is a youth-focused publication about Latin music, culture, and entertainment.

Rewire

https://rewire.news

If you're looking for independent, fact-based journalism about social issues such as reproductive rights and LGBTQ rights, Rewire is the place to go.

Scarleteen

http://www.scarleteen.com

Scarleteen hosts the internet's most thorough and inclusive information about sexuality and relationships geared toward teens.

Teen Vogue

https://www.teenvogue.com

Teen Vogue covers politics, movies, fashion, and all other topics teens care about, with an eye on diversity and inclusion.

INDEX

abortion, 82, 89–91, 105
  history of, 89
  hotline, 89
  medication, 89
  reasons for, 85, 90
  surgical, 89
abuse, 33
  emotional, 97–98
  helping friends with, 102
  hotline for, 97
  LGBTQ and, 27, 101
  loveisrespect, 97
  physical, 62, 69, 97–98
  signs of, 100–101
  substance, 31, 100, 104
agender, 14, 22, 25
anatomy
  biological, 14–15, 22
  gender and, 22
  infographics, 16–17, 19
anorexia, 40
artificial insemination, 14, 84
asexuality, 24

Bechdel Test, 36
binge eating, 40
biological sex, 14, 22
birth control, 50–51, 80,
    82, 86
  condoms, 85–87
  douching, 54, 85
  hormonal implant, 88
  hormonal shot, 88
  infographic, 88
  intrauterine devices
    (IUDs), 50–51, 86–87
  the Pill, 50–51, 86–87
  Plan B One-Step, 87
  rhythm method, 85
  tubal ligation, 88
  vaginal rings, 50–51, 88

vasectomy, 88–89
  withdrawal method, 84
bisexuality, 7, 24–25, 27, 36
body shame
  counseling, 39
  dieting, 39
  in media, 37
  social media, 38, 71
breaking up, 69–70, 92,
    102–105
breasts, 9, 23, 50, 59, 85
  development of, 46–47,
    49, 51
  hair on, 28–29
  shape and size of, 13, 20,
    28–29, 35, 38, 80
bulimia, 40

catcalling, 7
circumcision, 18, 54
cisgender, 14, 25, 27
clitoris
  infographics, 16–17
  and sexual pleasure, 17,
    76–78
coercion, 92.
  See sexual assault
consent, 7, 15, 66, 80, 89, 96
  definition of, 4–8, 91
  guidelines, 8–10
  physical, 10
  saying no, 9, 65
  sexting and, 12, 72–74
  verbal, 9, 78, 84
counseling, 23, 39, 41, 89–90,
    97, 102–103
  (see also mental health)

dating. See relationships
discrimination, 32–34
  ableism, 32–33, 37

classism, 32
  dating and, 33
  homophobia, 26–28,
    32–33, 37
  racism, 32–33, 36–37
  sexism, 31–36
  speaking up against,
    33–34
  transphobia, 32
douching, 54, 85

emotional labor, 34–35
emotions, 23–24, 45, 47, 70,
    96–99, 103
  expressing, 39, 62,
    64–65, 74
  masculinity and, 30–31,
    34
  sex and, 10, 75
erections, 18–19

female anatomy
  cervix, 14–17, 49, 57, 84,
    89
  clitoris, 16–17, 76–78
  hymen, 17
  labia majora, 15–17
  labia minora, 15–17
  ovaries, 14, 16, 23, 46–48,
    50, 88
  urethra, 16–17, 54
  uterus, 15–17, 23, 47–50,
    84, 87–89
  vagina, 14–17, 49–50,
    54–55, 57–59, 77–79,
    84–89
  vulva, 14–18, 20, 54–58, 77
feminism, 32

gender-confirmation surgery,
    23, 47

gender expression, 7, 20–22, 27
    androgynous, 21
    butch, 21, 27
    feminine, 20–21, 22, 35
    femme, 21
    masculine, 20–21, 22
gender fluid, 22, 25
gender identity, 14, 22, 25, 27–28, 32
genderqueer, 14
gender stereotypes, 27, 31–32
genitalia, 12, 51, 53–54
    gender and, 13–15, 22
    infographics, 16–17, 19
    sex and, 9, 56–58, 75–76, 79–80

heterosexism, 26
heterosexuality, 21, 24–27, 95
hormones, 14, 22, 50, 64, 87–88
    estrogen, 23, 48, 87
    gonadotropin, 44
    norepinephrine, 95
    progesterone, 48, 87
    progestin, 87
    puberty and, 18, 44–48
    testosterone, 23, 47
hotlines
    abortion, 89
    abuse, 97

illnesses and infections, 16, 39–40, 47, 51, 54, 59, 85
    cold sores, 55–56
    mononucleosis, 56
    sexually transmitted infections (STIs), 56–60
    urinary tract infections (UTIs), 54–55
    yeast infections, 55, 60

infographics
    birth control efficacy, 88
    clitoral anatomy, 17
    genitalia, 16, 19
intersex, 14–15

Kinsey, Alfred, 24
Kinsey Scale, 24–25

lubricants, 20, 78–79, 83

male anatomy
    foreskin, 18, 54
    penis, 12, 14, 16, 18–20, 46, 54, 56–58, 72, 76–80, 84, 86
    scrotum, 19, 46
    testes, 14, 19–20, 46, 89
    urethra, 19, 54
    vas deferens, 19–20, 89
masturbation, 76–77
    fantasies, 77
    myths about, 77
menstruation, 13, 16–17, 29, 47–51, 55, 86
    amenorrhea, 47
    definition of, 47
    endometrium, 48, 50–51
    menses, 47
    ovulation, 29, 48, 87
    premenstrual syndrome, 49–50
mental health, 30–31
    counseling, 23, 41, 89–90, 97, 102–103
    exercise, 41, 47, 50, 104
    food, 40–41, 47, 70, 104
    self-care, 41, 96
    social media and, 42, 71
negging, 39, 67
nonbinary, 14, 21–23, 47, 101
non-monogamy, 93

orgasm, 77, 79–81, 89

pansexuality, 25
period. See menstruation
pop culture
    body shame and, 35–40
    LGBTQ, 26, 35–37
    sexism and, 31–32
porn, 73, 80
pregnancy, 14, 17, 48–49, 58, 77, 78, 80, 82–83, 84, 86–87, 89–90, 95, 105
    signs of, 85
premenstrual syndrome (PMS)
    symptoms of, 49–50
    treatment for, 50–51
puberty, 18, 44–52
    acne, 45
    body hair, 15, 45
    delayed, 51
    height, 44
    mood swings, 45

relationships, 35, 94–95, 102–104
    communication, 43, 61–65, 68
    consent, 5–12, 65
    jealousy, 96–97
    open, 93
    red flags, 12, 98–101
    sex and, 76, 79–81, 83, 91–92
    social media and, 33–34, 70–71

sex, 5, 19, 24, 26, 54–55, 75, 79–83, 95, 98
    communication, 53, 64–66, 68, 75–76, 83–84
    consent, 8–11, 91

sexually transmitted infections(STIs),56–60
types of, 16–17, 20, 77–79
sexual assault, 91–92
sexual harassment, 7, 69, 98
obsession, 96–97
stalking, 96
sexuality, 4, 11, 26, 33, 38, 61, 75, 77, 95
Kinsey Scale, 24–25
spectrum of, 24–25
sexuallytransmittedinfections (STIs), 56–60
AIDS (acquired immunodeficiency syndrome), 59–60
chlamydia, 57–58, 60
genital herpes, 58

gonorrhea, 58
HIV (human immunodeficiencyvirus), 59–60
human papillomavirus (HPV), 57
prevention of, 56–57
syphilis, 58
testing for, 57, 60
treatment for, 57–59
sexual orientation, 7, 23–27, 32–33, 52, 59, 78
shaving, 15, 29, 45, 51–52, 64
social media, 29, 71–72, 96–98
relationships and, 71, 102
research on, 38, 42
street harassment, 7

transgender, 7, 14, 21, 25, 36
gender-confirmation surgery, 23, 47
hormones, 23, 47
misgendering, 22, 62
pronouns, 22–23, 62–63
transitioning, 23

unhealthy relationships, 98
helping friends with, 102
signs of, 99–101

values, 5–8, 11, 31, 61, 64, 81–82, 91, 96
virginity, 73, 82

PHOTO ACKNOWLEDGMENTS

Design Elements: mustafahacalaki/Getty Images; Artemisia1508/Getty Images; jvillustrations/Shutterstock.com. Laura Westlund/Independent Picture Service, pp. 16, 17, 19, 88.

ABOUT THE AUTHOR

SARAH MIRK is a social justice-focused writer and artist who loves to read, draw comics, make zines, pet dogs, and learn about the world. She began her career as a journalist for alternative weekly newspapers the *Stranger* and the *Portland Mercury,* where she covered political issues and numerous colorful characters. She then worked as the online editor of national feminism and pop culture nonprofit Bitch Media. In that role, she edited and published critical work from dozens of writers, ran social media pages with a reach of 1.5 million readers, and hosted the engaging feminist podcast *Popaganda,* whose ten thousand listeners tuned into episodes on topics ranging from environmental justice to reproductive rights. She moved on to become a contributing editor at graphic journalism website the Nib, where she writes and edits nonfiction comics about history, politics, and identity. She is the author of the book *Sex from Scratch: Making Your Own Relationship Rules* and the sci-fi graphic novel *Open Earth.* Mirk holds a degree in history, with honors, from Grinnell College. She identifies as queer and cisgender and lives in Portland, Oregon, with her partner. You can follow her work on Twitter or Instagram @sarahmirk. She always welcomes questions and good ideas.